Fabric Memory Books

Italy 2003

Color

Fabric Memory Books

Techniques, Projects, Inspiration

Lesley Riley

A LARK/CHAPELLE BOOK

A Division of Sterling Publishing Co., Inc.
New York

A Lark/Chapelle Book

Chapelle, Ltd., Inc.
P.O. Box 9255, Ogden, UT 84409
(801) 621-2777 · (801) 621-2788 Fax
e-mail: chapelle@chapelleltd.com
Web site: www.chapelleltd.com

10 9 8 7 6 5 4 3 2 1

First Edition

Published by Lark Books, A Division of
Sterling Publishing Co., Inc.
387 Park Avenue South, New York, N.Y. 10016

© 2006, Lesley Riley

Distributed in Canada by Sterling Publishing,
c/o Canadian Manda Group, 165 Dufferin Street
Toronto, Ontario, Canada M6K 3H6

Distributed in the United Kingdom by GMC Distribution Services,
Castle Place, 166 High Street, Lewes, East Sussex, England BN7 1XU

Distributed in Australia by Capricorn Link (Australia) Pty Ltd.,
P.O. Box 704, Windsor, NSW 2756 Australia

Manufactured in China

All rights reserved

ISBN 13: 978-1-57990-985-7
ISBN 10: 1-57990-985-X

For information about custom editions, special sales, premium and corporate purchases, please contact Sterling Special Sales Department at 800-805-5489 or specialsales@sterlingpub.com.

Concept Editor:

Jennifer Gibbs

Production Editors:

Dave MacFarlane

Jennifer Gibbs

Book Designer:

828, Inc.

Photographer:

Zac Williams

Art is our memory of love. The most an artist can do through their work is say, let me show you what I have seen, what I have loved and perhaps you will see it and love it too.

~ Annie Bevan

For my sister, Katie, and my friends, Christine, Nina, Pokey, Claudine, and Judi. I would not be able to do all that I do without these wonderful women in my life.

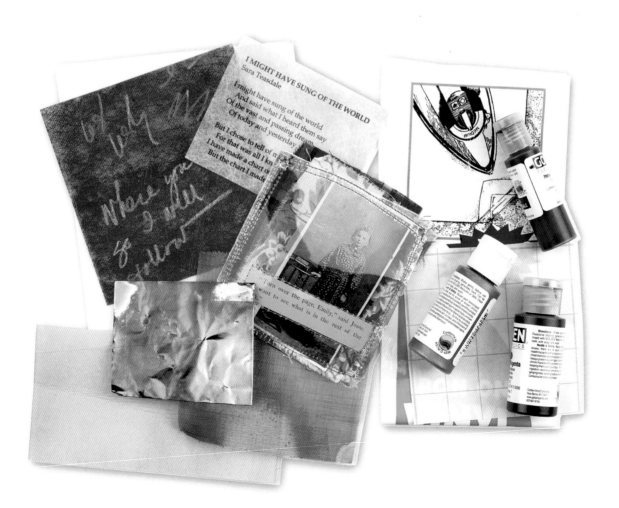

Table of Contents

Introduction

Once Upon a Time

Reading those first stories with my mom gave me even more than a love for words and pictures—it gave me a love for books themselves.

> There are perhaps no days of childhood we loved so fully as those spent with a favorite book.
>
> ~Marcel Proust

One of the first things my mother shared with me was a love of reading. I still have the very first books she gave me, the ones that I learned to "read" back to her, having memorized every word. From Margaret Wise Brown's *Goodnight Moon* and Dr. Seuss's *Gerald McBoing Boing*, to the magnificent *Harold and the Purple Crayon* by Crockett Johnson, books were my first true love.

While I recognized the magic of books early on, it took me longer to fall in love with fabric. In 1971, I created my first quilt, and I've had a beautiful relationship with this amazing medium ever since. Fabric sparks my imagination and fires the stories in my heart. From a love for fabric, books, and the stories they tell, it was a short leap to a fascination with fabric books. Whether a page is made of paper or fabric, it offers a tactile experience and the beautiful promise of what it could contain. Artists have been combining paper and fabric into books for many years—telling stories with paragraphs of pattern, words of thread, and punctuation of trim and ephemera. Now it's your turn. You already have what you need to get started: hands, eyes, imagination. This book will show you what they can help you do.

Your level of experience with book-making will probably affect how you approach this book. If you're an experienced bookmaker, it's likely you will want to go straight to Part Two and get started on projects. If you're a newcomer, Part One will introduce you to the materials, tools, and page construction methods I've used, as well as provide an overview of printing photos on fabric, making photo transfers, and telling stories through images. When you're ready to try a project, flip through Part Two and review the book-binding methods described at the beginning of each section to help you choose a method to try.

This book includes instructions for twenty-four fabric memory books, but please consider them to be suggestions only. Improvise, alter, or adjust them to meet your own needs and desires. Please give yourself permission to do your own thing. While extra attention to details that show and details that affect the durability of a book can enhance your satisfaction with the project when it's done, you don't need formal bookbinding experience to make fabric

memory books (I didn't when I started). That's what makes this medium so great—quilters, sewers, mixed-media artists, and collagers can join book-makers on common ground while maintaining their unique perspectives. I share techniques and ideas that have worked for me, but there are many other valid approaches, some of which are still waiting to be discovered. I encourage you to just dive in, rather than worry about doing something the "right" way. It's more fun, and you may love the results even more if you pay more attention to the overall design and content than to precise measurements. And if a project has imperfections? Work with them. Nine times out of ten, only you will consider them flaws. Others will recognize them as the mark of the human hand that makes your work extraordinary.

BOOK
smarts

Transform a mistake into a stroke of design genius. For instance, if a line you intended to sew straight turns out crooked, try sewing another crooked line, turning the crooked line into an intentional design element.

Part One:

Bookmaking Basics

Art is about presenting the possibility
of a different way of thinking.

~ Josephine Le Grice

Materials
Old and New

With a plethora of magazines, TV shows, and
websites at our fingertips, it's easy to feel that
everything interesting has already been done.
Fortunately, artists are magicians. We can turn
ordinary materials into unique objects of beauty
and wonder. It's our job to see the world with new
eyes every day. Creating original art really is as
simple as asking a series of "what if" questions:
"What if I used this as a binding instead of that?"
"What if a book was shaped like a star?" "What if
my pages were vintage textiles?" To be a book
artist, you must ask yourself the questions that are
the starting point for every great invention. It's easy.
Try it right now. Ask yourself a "what if" question
about a shape, a color, a medium, or anything else
that might lead to a concept for your next project.

Old Materials

One of the best parts of creating is finding new uses for old materials. Before you go to the craft store to buy more stuff, spur your creative abilities (and save your money) by taking another look at what you already have. Whether it's leftovers from other projects or precious items rescued from a flea market, you're sure to discover useable materials if you scour the house with open eyes and a fabric book in mind. I offer the following list as a place to get started; by all means, let your imagination range beyond it.

Board books The solid cardboard and limited number of pages in a children's board book makes it perfect for holding fabrics, photos, and mementoes. The diminutive size of the typical board book offers a great opportunity to use leftover bits of favorite fabrics and trims.

Buttons Look at worn or outdated clothing for these precious gems. They can serve as bold or delicate accents, dramatic focal points or as functional and decorative bindings. Your buttons don't have to match, even in size. Mixing color, shape, and size is another way to add a unique touch to your book.

Grommets and eyelets Artists have recently discovered what the makers of tents, sails, and shower curtains have known for eons: grommets and eyelets are nifty little items. They reinforce the material around holes, preventing accidental tears while providing a clean, finished look, which is ideal for preparing pages for binding with ribbon, rings, or fabric strips. Eyelets range in size from $1/8"$ to $1/2"$. Grommets, which are larger, typically develop a lovely patina when exposed to flame.

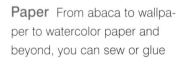

Paper From abaca to wallpaper to watercolor paper and beyond, you can sew or glue

any weight of paper into a fabric book. Try painting the paper then collaging on some fabric. To make delicate papers sturdy enough to be sewn, apply a coat or two of soft gel acrylic medium.

Rug hooking canvas The open-squared canvas used to make rugs is a strong and interesting material for fabric books. Use it to make a great cover or cut it into narrow strips and tie it with ribbon to create a decorative edge.

Sheer fabric Long the stuff of little girls' dreams, tulle and other sheer fabrics bring ethereal beauty to a fabric book. Make see-through pages with layers of sheer fabric or create a color "glaze" using a translucent sheer over a solid page.

Sticks A stick gives a fabric book some spine. It can be covered or exposed, purely functional or decorative as well. Anything that is the length of your book and has the needed strength can serve as a spine. Look for pencils, paintbrushes, rulers, and chopsticks, to name just a few possibilities.

Used books Used bookstores are bursting with old books that no one wants. What's a fabric book artist to do? Turn them into art, of course. Take a hardcover book, replace the original pages with fabric pages, and transform the cover with fabric. Voila!

Vintage textiles Women of yesteryear often added beauty to their lives by embroidering everyday linens. Why not add some of this beauty to your life now by finding ways to use vintage scarves, handkerchiefs, napkins, doilies, and other textiles in a fabric memory book?

Same old eyes, same old world but the difference is how you look at what is in front of you, not what it is.

~ Lister Sinclair

BOOK smarts When confronted with familiar materials, ask yourself a "what if" question to help you recognize how it can be used in an entirely new way.

New Materials

Loving fabric doesn't stop me from flirting with any other material I can take a needle to. Combining different textures and surfaces creates rich and interesting books. The contrasts of hard and soft, rigid and flowing, plant and mineral, make for a more visual and tactile sensory experience. Some of the materials not normally associated with fabric bookmaking can make intriguing substitutes for traditional fabric book materials. Look to the Internet and your favorite craft store for help in finding non-traditional materials.

Copper mesh When fine copper wires are woven, they form a mesh that behaves like fabric. Tear it along the grain and finish by double-folding the rough edges or covering them with a fabric binding. To change the color of the metal, apply a hot flame—the heat yields beautiful shades of color from gold to red and purple to blue.

Copper sheet Any sheet of metal thin enough to cut with regular household scissors is suitable for machine sewing. While craft metal is available in a number of colors, copper sheets can also be re-colored using fire. Emboss, crimp, and pattern these thin metal sheets to further embellish your pages.

Fluid acrylic paint This richly saturated, liquid version of acrylic tube paint works well on fabric, interfacing, and paper. For fabric, I find fluid acrylics are better than dyes because they can be applied more spontaneously. They're versatile, too, permitting you to apply deep, undiluted color or thin, translucent washes. To set fluid acrylics, apply the heat of an iron. What's even better for fabric artists is that light washes of the paint don't change the feel of the fabric and thick layers change it only a little.

Interfacing Interfacing comes in several weights, from featherweight to extra heavy. For fabric bookmaking, use medium and heavyweight interfacing, depending on the rigidity needed. It is a paintable surface, accepts transfers, and takes ink from a variety of pens, making it perfect for fabric book pages.

Mica Mica is an amalgam of minerals mined in thick multi-layered sheets that can be separated into translucent sheets thin enough for machine sewing. Carefully peel off as many layers as you can without it falling apart. Layer the mica over photos for a glass-like effect, or enclose fabric and photos between sheets and stitch around the edges to create a book page.

Spun-bonded paper Sold in brands such as Tyvek, this material is a wonderful surface for fabric book pages. It can be cut, glued, sewn, and colored. It also shrinks and bubbles when heat is applied, adding dimension to collage and fabric design.

Spun-bonded polyester This non-woven material is ideal for fabric book artists. Lightweight and water resistant, it can be painted, heat set, etched, sewn, and written on, all without fraying or unraveling. Look for brands such as Lutradur, which are marketed specifically to artists.

Vinyl Iron-on vinyl makes a great cover for a fabric book as it can be wiped of dirt and water and its sturdy surface resists wear and tear. Use it to laminate your fabric book covers simply by following the manufacturer's instructions.

Tools of the Craft

Chances are you already have many if not all of the following tools. While some are absolute necessities for bookmaking, and some are optional, all of them will make your fabric bookmaking adventures easier.

Awl This long, thin tool is handy for punching holes in fabric layers.

Burnisher Any smooth, hard tool such as a bone folder or a spoon can be used to rub (burnish) a photo in the transfer process.

Clamps Use these to hold a stack of fabric pages in place while you're working.

Craft knife Also called a utility knife, this tool is great for cutting non-fabric materials. I find a #11 blade is ideal.

Cutting mat This specially designed mat protects a work surface without damaging the blades of your craft knife and rotary cutter.

Glues To adhere trim, three dimensional items, and so on, select a type made for the materials you're working with—fabric glue, craft glue, clear silicone glue, wood glue, etc.

Iron and ironing board Have these items close to your work area for quickly and safely smoothing wrinkles, setting creases, and applying iron-on fusible.

Iron-on fusible Also known as "fusible," this material is a type of interfacing that reacts to the heat of an iron to bond fabrics without sewing.

Japanese screw punch This small, hand-held tool punches clean holes through a variety of materials, including fabric, mica, copper mesh, and copper sheets.

Marking tool Have chalk, a pencil, or a disappearing marker on hand for marking layouts and reference points on your materials.

Measuring tape or ruler I prefer 24" clear acrylic rulers that provide a straight edge and the ability to see the fabric underneath.

Needles An assortment pack of needles can cover most of your hand-sewing requirements.

Paintbrushes One-inch foam brushes are inexpensive and versatile tools for applying fluid acrylic paints and glue.

Paperclips Have several on hand to hold together materials that can't be pinned while you work, such as delicate mica sheets.

Permanent pens and markers Use these to write sentiments, quotes, and journaling on fabric.

Pliers To pull needles through fabric, a pair of small, needle-nose pliers work best.

Rotary cutter Looking something like a pizza slicer, a rotary cutter can help you cut faster and more precisely than scissors.

Sewing machine While there are many models with elaborate functions available today, a simple, inexpensive machine that sews straight stitches is all you really need to speed your book-sewing.

Scissors Dedicate a pair to use only on fabric to keep the blades sharp.

Straight pins Use these to hold fabric in place and mark positions while you work.

Thread A cotton or cotton-poly blend will serve most needs, but you may want to have heavier threads on hand for securing heavier elements and thicker bindings.

Photographic Memories

Photographs are our silent records of the past. Whether the people, places, or things photographs capture are well known or long forgotten, they hold an undeniable magic. Choosing, enhancing, printing, and transferring photographs are integral parts of creating fabric memory books. Thankfully, you don't have to be a skilled photographer or have photographs in perfect condition to include them in your book—you can enhance the composition and quality of your vintage portraits and contemporary snapshots.

Just as "a picture is worth a thousand words," the cropping of the picture will determine what those words shall be.

~ Gordon Hull

Enhancing Photographs

The most important tool you can have for enhancing photographs is a computer. If you have a digital camera, you can download pictures directly into your computer; if you're working from hard copy (non-digital) photographs, you also need a scanner to turn them into digital images that can be manipulated on the computer.

A variety of computer programs allow you to change digital images. If you're cost conscious, remember that most digital cameras and scanners come with software that enables you to do basic photo editing, and some programs are even offered free on the Internet. Whichever one you choose, look for one that enables you to crop, enlarge, reduce, enhance, and change the color of your images.

Photo Editing Terms

To edit photos, use the functions listed below to adjust and re-adjust the various aspects of the image until you get the look you want. Play around with the various options and take risks. When you are happy with the results, be sure to save the new image.

Basic Photo Editing Functions
- **Crop** Allows you to remove distracting background elements to create a focus on the main subject.
- **Resolution** Refers to the quality of the saved image; for best printing quality, convert photos to "high resolution" or 300 dots per inch (dpi).
- **Contrast** Use this option to brighten or deepen lights and darks.
- **Color** Use this option to strengthen or fade color.
- **Brighten** Lighten up the entire photo, especially important when printing on fabric.
- **Hue/Saturation** This option allows you to manipulate the strength of color and may reveal hidden colors.

Advanced Photo Editing Functions
- **Selective color** More sophisticated programs allow you to adjust each color individually, such as to remove a yellow tint from white areas.
- **Curves** This option enables you to adjust the tonal range of shadows, mid-tones, and highlights.
- **Filters** Use filters to define edges, sharpen or blur images, erase flaws, etc.
- **Red-eye Reducer** This function allows you to get rid of those otherworldly irises.

Printing Photos on Fabric

Chances are you do not want to use original photos in your projects. Rather than printing copies of photos on paper, print them on fabric to add a beautiful dimension to your fabric memory books. Advances in the technology and materials involved have opened a range of delightful possibilities and made copying and printing photos at home easier than ever. Even better, printers, inks, and other materials are being developed and refined continually to make printing on fabric easier, cheaper, and, most importantly, permanent.

BOOK
smarts

Whatever method you use to print photos onto fabric, you will need to lighten and brighten the images before you print. Fabric absorbs the ink differently than paper, causing photos to appear darker on the fabric than they do on your monitor.

There are several options available for printing on fabric. For many, the most convenient option is to buy inkjet-ready fabric that has been pre-treated with a chemical that bonds inks to the fabric. With ink-jet ready fabric, the inks will not wash or fade away, but the fabric colors are limited to white and off-white.

A more versatile and less costly option is to prepare your own fabric by soaking it in a special chemical solution. This is the best option if you want to print on colored fabrics or want to save money. You'll also need to add a backing to the fabric to enable it to feed through the printer. (Inkjet-ready fabric is already backed.) A popular method is to iron freezer paper, shiny-side down, to the fabric, but paper-backed iron-on fusible also works. If you have trouble with your fabric feeding smoothly through the printer, cut off the two leading corners at a 45-degree angle to help your fabric load into the printer more easily.

A third option is to print directly onto fabric using pigment ink. Because pigment inks are not water-based, they do not require a pre-treated fabric. An added benefit is that pigments inks are water resistant and fade resistant for up to one hundred years. Just keep in mind that for best results, you must allow the pigment print to dry thoroughly before exposing it to water. Iron a pigment-ink print only enough to smooth the fabric; heat does not help the ink to set, and excessive heat may damage the print.

Transferring Photos onto Fabric

When you want something more unusual than the look of a conventional photo printed on fabric, try a transfer instead. The act of transferring photos to fabric has always felt like a kind of magic to me because the results are always a surprise. The process of transferring printer inks to fabric leaves broken, blurred, or incomplete areas, creating an ancient, mysterious aura that adds another layer of depth to a fabric memory book. While there are various methods for transferring photos, I find that I get the look I want with the least expense using my two favorite inkjet-based methods: acrylic medium transfers and water transfers.

For an acrylic medium transfer, you use liquid matte medium to transfer an image that has been reverse-printed (a mirror image) onto a transparency with an inkjet printer. Be sure to get liquid, not gel, matte medium because the added wetness is necessary to penetrate fabric. Working on a non-porous surface, evenly brush just enough matte medium onto the fabric to wet it, but not enough to saturate it. Place the transparency ink-side-down onto the fabric, burnish it, then slowly peel back the corners to peek at the results. If necessary, stop peeling and burnish more before removing the transparency.

For a water transfer, print an image onto glossy photo paper using an inkjet printer, spray a mist of water over the image until it is evenly damp, then place it facedown on the fabric. Using a burnisher, rub the back of the paper thoroughly. Peel back the paper slowly to check the results. If necessary, mist with more water and burnish again. To finish, spray the image with a workable fixative spray to set the inks.

BOOK smarts   Regardless of which method of transfer you use, always print your images as color photos, even if they are black and white. Printing in color reproduces more subtle color gradations from your original photo.

> *It always amazes me to think that every house on every street is full of so many stories; so many triumphs and tragedies, and all we see are yards and driveways.*
>
> ~ Glenn Close

The Art of Storytelling

As I discussed in my first book, *Quilted Memories*, a story can be told entirely through images. When you create your own fabric memory books, chances are that pictures will be your primary focus, and that words, if there are any, will be used to embellish or document. Whatever your approach, keep in mind that some stories are about feelings and impressions rather than events. Such books aren't about saying what happened as much as they are about expressing different moods. Each page can deepen the same mood or alter it, depending on what story you want to tell.

To create an amazing book, let the story you want to tell guide your design decisions. Choose fabric with a look and feel that supports the theme or mood you want to convey. You may even want the fabric itself to be the main subject of your book, like *Natural Resources* (page 72), which presents a different heirloom textile on every page.

When telling your tale, try to engage all the viewers' senses. Of course, you'll aim to catch their eyes with interesting color and composition, but there are many other ways to intrigue a reader. Experiment with ways to incorporate sound through elements such as crinkly page materials or bells. Make the pages irresistible with textures that beckon to the fingertips. Even size and shape can enhance the storytelling. A tiny book can be a pleasure to hold, while a big book fairly shouts its importance. An unusual shape, such as a teddy bear, can evoke a smile, making a person so primed for delight that she simply must open the book and see what's inside.

The Story of One Book

As you work, keep your imagination ready for inspiration by staying open to the possibilities that arise. For example, I got the idea for the book *Land of Milk and Honey* (page 36) while playing around with something called sequin waste—the holey plastic sheets manufacturers are left with after they punch out sequins. I was painting over a piece, using it as a stencil, when it occurred to me that it looked like honeycomb. From there I envisioned a book filled with honey-toned gold and yellow fabrics, layers of textures, and rich creamy white. A phone call got my grandchildren working on a photo of them sporting milk mustaches while I collected fabrics and ephemera to enhance my vision. Though the idea for the book came in a flash of serendipity, each element of the final product was carefully chosen to reinforce the theme.

BOOK
smarts   When creating a design for a book, consider how color, texture, sound, size, and shape
can be combined to support the overall concept for the story you want to tell.

Composition

Once you have a sense of the overall story or theme of your book, it's time to plan the composition of the pages. One way to understand the principles of composition is entirely intuitive. Pretend you're at a conference event. There's quiet music in the background, setting the mood. The room is full of pleasant chatter and subtle whispers when the speaker steps to the podium, drawing all eyes to the front. Now think about a fabric memory book: your focal point is like the speaker, your fabric is like the music, and the other elements you choose are like the various levels of conversation that murmur just below the surface. While you want participants to experience the whole room and a sense of connection with everyone in it, ultimately you want their eyes to return to that podium.

When creating a fabric book, you first need to choose your background music—the fabric for your pages. The color and texture should complement the theme of the book and not overpower the artwork that will go into the book. In your fabric book, each page or page spread will have a focal point, usually a photograph or image. I usually put images in the lower left or right portion of each page, leaving room for other elements at the top. Next, add the conversation and whispers of fabric snippets, pieces of vintage lace, other photos, or ephemera. I define whispers as tiny elements that add interest to the page.

Another way to understand composition is more analytical. Consider how a living thing such as a tree achieves balance. What keeps it from toppling over? Does the trunk bend one way and heavy branches go another way? Are the left and right sides symmetrical? Do the roots (at your best guess) go as deep into the earth as the branches reach into the sky? Now look at a landscape. There's the earth, grounding us, balanced by an open sky overhead—substance and space. What is it about the combination that makes it calming to see?

In art as in nature, we tend to prefer balance. Distribute the elements in your layout so that the eye isn't stuck to just one area, but rather can take in the whole composition on its way to the focal point. The color, shape, size, and texture of a design element will make it seem heavier or lighter, with heavier elements slowing or stopping the eye more readily. To create compositions that don't topple over, place heavier elements toward the bottom and include some open area, or white space, to allow the eye to rest. Prevent parts of the layout from being cut off by connecting diagonal lines with vertical and horizontal lines the way branches connect to trees.

a little shopping in Florence

my handsome gondolier

Each page of *Italy 2003* constitutes a complete event, with a speaker, background music, conversation, and whispers. On the page on the right, the large photo is the focal point, while other elements such as secondary photos and snippets of fabric murmur in the background, with a shout of cheerful orange ribbon tying the composition together.

BOOK smarts

The various characteristics of a design element work interdependently to make it appear "heavy" or "light." For instance, a small, black square may seem heavier than a very large, pastel circle, whereas a large gray button will seem heavier than small gray one. For a more detailed discussion of design elements and principles, please see my book, *Quilted Memories* (Sterling/Chapelle, 2005).

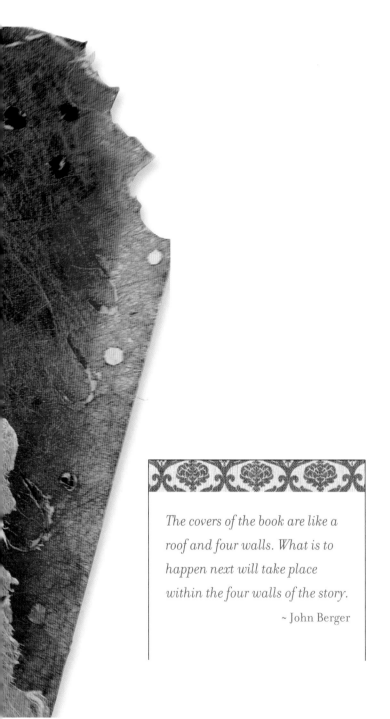

Fabric Bookmaking Techniques

Technically speaking, there are three basic components to most bookmaking projects: the cover, the pages, and how you hold them all together. In Part Two, I describe—and show you—various ways to accomplish the latter at the beginning of each chapter. Here, I'll tell you what you need to know about covers and pages.

Though the cover is the first thing a reader sees, it should be the last thing you create. Why? Because after you create the book that goes with it, you may change your mind. Maybe the theme or the design has shifted. Maybe the size turns out to be all wrong. You need to allow room for the creative process to offer you surprises, allowing your art to retain the same spontaneous quality of that first flash of inspiration. Adhering too rigidly to a plan can extinguish the creative spark that sets one work apart from another. The projects in Part Two have a variety of cover styles that range from simply being a book's first and last pages to being created separately to not even having a cover at all.

As far as page construction methods go, all of the projects in *Fabric Memory Books* were made from a combination of four page types: single-sided pages, double-sided pages, double-sided pages back-to-back, and folded pages. From these, countless fabric designs can begin.

The covers of the book are like a roof and four walls. What is to happen next will take place within the four walls of the story.

~ John Berger

BOOK smarts   You don't need a sewing machine to make great fabric memory books. Many can be created just by folding pages accordion-style or by binding them with glue or iron-on fusible. Of the projects in Part Two that require sewing, most can be stitched by hand.

Single-sided pages can be used to achieve various effects. Here, a woman from *Follow* (page 118) peers into a space where the ethereal shape of the dancer on the following page shows through.

Single-Sided Pages

With single-sided page construction, you work on the front of a page only, leaving the back blank. While it's by far the easiest page construction method, don't be fooled—the results can be anything but simplistic. You can bind individual pages as in *Natural Resources* (page 72) and *Fabric Journal* (page 70), attach them to an altered book like *Land of Milk & Honey* (page 36), or keep them loose but collected in a scrapbook or fabric box, as they are in *Home* (page 42). You can even create a whole book from a single page, like *How I Color My World* (page 38).

Double-Sided Pages

Take single-sided pages a step further by joining two of them back-to-back after you have collaged on them but before you bind the book. To create the pages in *Stone Angels* (page 67), I machine stitched a fabric collage on one side of each page. After deciding which pages I wanted to face each other, I stitched them together in the correct sequence to create my double-sided pages. You can also use double-sided pages for an accordion-folded book like *Italy 2003* (page 50).

Depending on which book construction technique you use, double-sided pages can give you the opportunity to create compositions across two-page spreads. For this spread from *Family* (page 108), coordinating fabrics connect individual photos of a couple.

Folded-Page Construction

In folded-page construction, a single piece of fabric is folded to create individual pages and, in some cases, the covers, too. One example is *Be* (page 40), which is a special type of book with folded pages called an eight-fold book (page 34).

Most fabrics do not have enough body for folded-page construction. Suitable fabrics include those that have some stiffness, like cotton duck, canvas, and felt, but that aren't too thick, as many decorator-weight fabrics are. More flexible fabrics can be used if you stitch or fuse two pieces of fabric together with medium or heavyweight interfacing between them, as I did with *Starbook* (page 60). Yet another alternative is to skip fabric altogether

and just use interfacing. The heavyweight interfacings are stiff enough to make crisp folds and firm pages without adding bulk, and though you can leave interfacing pages white, you'll probably love how it drinks up the colors of fluid acrylics or dye.

Signature Construction

The tricky part of fabric bookmaking comes when you use signature page construction. Put simply, a signature is formed when you stack multiple pages, attach them at the midline, and fold them in half. Many paper books (such as this one) are made of numerous signatures bound together inside a cover. The challenge of this method is that you need to plan your layouts with special care, designing each half of each side of the pages to fit the order in which they'll appear in the signature.

To form a signature with six spreads, stack three double-sided pages and bind them together by pinning or sewing through the stack along the midline. This will create twelve book pages that are half the size of those you originally started with, or six spreads. Each spread will be a combination of two halves of different original pages, with the left side of the spread being the front left of one original page and the right being the back right of another. (See Diagram 1).

The first step in creating signature pages is to cut material for double-sided pages that are twice as wide as the desired width of each finished page. Before you sew or fuse the front piece and back piece of each double-sided page together, pin them in place then stack each double-sided page into a signature. Test your book's layout by flipping through the stacked double-sided pages and see if you like the order. If you do, you are ready to create the artwork on each page.

Pin the material for each double-sided page, then stack and fold the pages to create the signature. As far as designing the pages, your options include working on each one while the pages are stacked and folded together, or taking apart the stack and working on each individually. If you do want to separate them, create a dummy (see the sidebar on page 31) and use the same numbering system on your pages as you use on the dummy. Write the page numbers on paper or fabric and pin each one to the corresponding page of the fabric book.

Usually, I unpin the pages but keep them stacked and folded so that I can work on both pages of a spread simultaneously to ensure that they relate to each other. This approach also enables me to add elements that travel across the spread.

Once you have collaged each page, stitch or fuse the four outer edges. Reassemble the double-sided pages in the correct order and stitch along the mid-line to create the finished signature, then bind each signature to the cover using one of the bookbinding techniques described in Part Two.

Making a Dummy

If creating a signature sounds too complicated, make a "dummy" to help you. A dummy is a mocked-up book layout that book and magazine publishers use when planning layouts.

1. Stack three pieces of paper and fold them in half.
2. Starting on the top page, label it R (right).
3. Open the top sheet and label the next two pages 1L and 1R, as in page 1, left and right.
4. Turn the page and number the next two pages 2L and 2R.
5. Continue numbering each spread consecutively.
6. Label the back page L for left.

Note: When combining two or more signatures, the front R of one signature will match up with the back L of another.

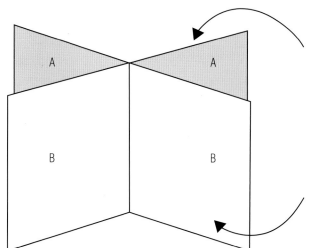

DIAGRAM 1. To form a signature, stack two or more sheets of material and bind them down the center to create eight or more single-sided pages. To make double-sided pages using signature construction, keep in mind that you will be stitching or fusing adjacent pages, so you will want to work on the back of "A" and the front of "B," as indicated by the arrows in this diagram.

Part Two:
A Library of Fabric Memory Books

Unbound and Prebound Books

As you'll see from the projects in this section, you can create an amazing fabric memory book without having to worry about a binding at all. One approach is to start with a children's board book as a sturdy "pre-bound" base on which to build your fabric book. Other approaches make a binding unnecessary because they use a single page for the entire book, as you'll see with the scroll book and the eight-fold book. And yet another option is to use a custom-built box to hold a portfolio of loose canvas pages. These projects enable beginners to focus on individual pages while giving experienced bookmakers plenty of room to express their creativity.

Altered Books

If you want a traditionally bound book but don't want to wrestle with the subtleties of binding methods, you can join the swelling ranks of altered book artists. For this approach, begin with a base book (children's board books are wonderfully sturdy), and apply your fabric collages to its pages using glue and other fixatives, as I did with *Land of Milk and Honey* (page 36).

Often, an altered book will not close completely. I like to think of such books as bursting with color and art, but if you are using a board book and you want it to close, split the outer spine by holding the book open, covers face-up. Using a craft knife, cut along the outer spine, avoiding the pages. If you will cover the book with a heavy fabric, leave the cut spine as is; otherwise, you can cover the split spine with a piece of duct tape for more security.

To attach the end of the scroll to a dowel, stitch or glue it in place or sandwich it between two half-round dowels and glue.

Scroll Books

Long before paper, long before bound books, there were scrolls—long stretches of animal hide or papyrus that rolled up for storage and transportation. The early Roman Empire saw the emergence of books bound along one edge, a brilliant invention that made finding a particular passage much easier. Today, we take bound books so much for granted, a scroll book can be an eyecatching alternative to the usual.

A scroll book is basically just one long page, either single- or double-sided, that has at least one end attached to and wrapped around a support. The book can be displayed on a wall, lying flat, or standing on supports, as *How I Color My World* (page 38) does. For storage of the finished scroll book, consider buying or creating a special container and decorating it to complement the scroll inside.

Eight-Fold Books

Like a scroll book, an eight-fold book is made from a single piece of material. Here, you use a rectangular piece of fabric or interfacing folded into eighths with strategically placed cuts along certain folds. The eight sections created by the folding become the front and back covers and six pages, as in *Be* (page 40).

A (front cover)	H (back cover)	G (page 6)	F (page 5)
B (page 1)	C (page 2)	D (page 3)	E (page 4)

DIAGRAM 1. When an eight-fold book is laid flat, the covers and pages 5 and 6 will appear upside down.

Strategically placed cuts and carefully oriented images for the pages in an eight-fold book enable the bookmaker to create a front cover, back cover, and three spreads from a single piece of material.

Although at first this form of construction may seem complicated, it's easy once you get the concept and the results can be very satisfying. To make an eight-fold book, begin with a stiff material like canvas, cotton duck, or interfacing that is four times as wide and two times as tall as you want the finished pages to be. For example, for a 5" x 7" book, cut the material to be 20" x 14". With the material placed before you so the rectangle is wider than it is tall, fold the material in half from top to bottom, then fold it evenly three times from side to side. Iron the material to set the folds, then open it and cut between the two middle rectangles (the dotted line in Diagram 1).

Now it's time to open the material again and create the artwork. Keep in mind that you will work on only one side of the material, flipping it upside down to work on some of the pages so they appear right side up in the finished book. For instance, pages A, H, G, and F in Diagram 1 will appear upside down until the book is folded.

Once you have collaged your pages, it's time to finish the book by folding it. First, fold down the top half so that pages B, C, D, and E are facing you. Open the top of the cut section where pages C/D and pages G/H meet. (See Diagram 2.) Push the other two sides of the book towards the center, forcing the fold at C/D and G/H outward. Fold again so A becomes the front cover and H becomes the back cover. Iron the edges of each pages to set the folds.

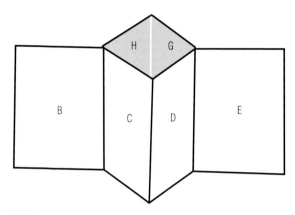

DIAGRAM 2. The slit cut between H/C and G/D allows you to pull pages C and D in one direction and G and H in the other. Note that A and F from Diagram 1 are hidden in this view.

Portfolio Books

When most of us think of books, we think of bound books. Yet the broader definition of "book" includes various ways of holding together a collection of pages or tablets. A boxed portfolio is one such approach that offers the bookmaker a wealth of creative possibilities. In this chapter, I share *Home* (page 42), a portfolio of single-sided pages made by different artists that I collected in a specially designed, fabric-covered box. What other ways to hold collections of loose pages can you think of?

BOOK
smarts

If the folded pages in an eight-fold book do not line up, adjust and sharpen the creases or smooth them down along the left side of the spine, pulling the right edges into place. Note that if you use a bulky fabric, the folded layers may be uneven due to the fabric thickness, but this may add to the charm of a handmade book.

LAND OF MILK & HONEY

This project is an altered book, meaning I applied my fabric and designs to a base book—in this case, a children's board book. Altered book art welcomes every skill, technique, tool, and embellishment you may have acquired over the years, making it a rich place for experimentation and play.

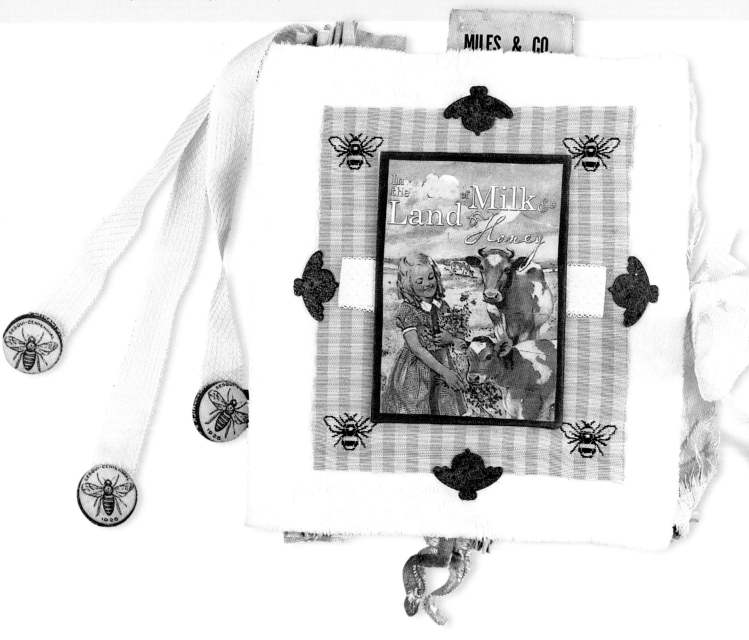

. . . unto a land flowing with milk and honey.

~ Exodus, 3:8

Art is the stored honey of the human soul.

~ Theodore Dreiser

Materials
Brush for glue · Buttons, charms, embellishments, ephemera · Children's board book · Fabrics, enough to cover pages, plus small scraps for collage · Photos on fabric or paper · Ribbon · Scissors or rotary cutter · Silicone glue · White fabric glue

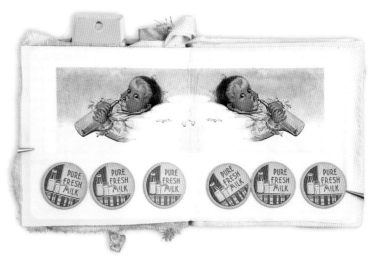

Method

1. Cut or tear the fabric slightly larger than the board book pages. Using fabric glue, adhere one piece across a two-page spread, glue one on each facing page, or use a combination of fabrics to cover the pages. Spread the glue thinly across each book page or spread. Avoid using so much glue that it bleeds through the fabric. Smooth out the fabric.

2. Leave the edges frayed or, to create a cleaner edge finish the edges by gluing (or sewing) them under, or wrapping the edge of one page around to the next, over or under the fabric on that page.

3. Collage the pages using fabric scraps and old pictures or images that have been transferred to cloth. Add additional bits of fabric, text, ephemera, buttons, etc. *Note: Add larger three-dimensional items when the book is almost complete so that they don't get dislodged.*

4. Glue one end of the ribbon tie to the front cover. Glue another piece of ribbon to the back cover, so that the two ends will tie the book closed.

5. With the book closed, use a brush to spread a thin layer of glue on the front cover. Place the cover fabric over it and smooth towards the spine. Put more glue on the spine plus about 1" of the back of the book; smooth the cover fabric over the spine and onto the back. Add glue to the rest of the back cover and smooth the fabric out to finish covering the book.

6. Add cover embellishments and/or ribbons, gluing them into place. Attach heavier items with silicone glue.

HOW I COLOR MY WORLD

How do you color your world? I started this scroll book by painting sheer interfacing with fluid acrylics without a plan. As a landscape emerged, I decided to make my children and grandchildren the flowers and trees and designed the book to stand upright in a curving display. To give the scroll more stability, I stacked three buttons, hiding washers in their recesses to give them extra weight.

You have your brush, you have your colors, you paint paradise, then in you go.

~ Nikos Kazantzakis

*I look out the window sometimes to seek the color of the shadows and the different greens
in the trees, but when I get ready to paint I just close my eyes and imagine a scene.*

~ Grandma Moses

Materials
Craft knife • Eighteen unpainted 1", two-hole buttons (or more for a longer scroll) • Fabric scraps • Foam brushes • Fluid acrylic paints • Heavyweight sheer interfacing or similar stiff fabric • Inkjet-ready fabric • Iron and ironing board • Iron-on fusible • Measuring tape or ruler • Paintbrushes • Photos • Scissors or rotary cutter • Sewing needle • Six washers to fit into button recesses • Straight pins • Thin dowels sized to fit into buttonholes • Thread • Wood glue • Wood sealer (optional) • Wood stain or paint (optional)

Method

1. Cut a length of interfacing long enough to fit your needs, plus 2".

2. Paint the interfacing with fluid acrylics and let it dry. *Note: The interfacing will dry slowly.*

3. Use a craft knife to cut a wooden dowel the height of the scroll plus 1". Repeat until you have enough dowels to place two every 6" to 8" plus a support on each end.

4. Paint the dowels with fluid acrylics to complement or contrast with the interfacing.

5. Scan, adjust, and print the selected photos on inkjet-ready fabric. Back the photos with iron-on fusible and cut them out.

6. Create a fabric and photo collage on the painted interfacing.

7. Stitch or fuse, the photos into place.

8. Paint, stain, or seal the buttons.

9. Place a washer in each recess of two buttons and stack a third one, on top.

10. Glue the buttons together. Align the buttonholes and verify that they are unobstructed by the washers by putting pins in the holes.

11. Glue a dowel into each buttonhole.

12. Fold over and stitch ½" of each end of the scroll to create a channel just large enough for one dowel.

13. Insert one dowel for support into the channel at each end.

14. Set the middle part of the scroll between the dowels in each support. Trim the dowels to the correct length and tie the top ends together with decorative thread.

BOOK smarts
Small as they are, the wood buttons and dowels in this project are an important part of the overall design scheme. Consider decorating them with decoupage, patina finishes, fabric or thread wraps, or wood stain.

BE

I made my first eight-fold book in a workshop with mixed-media artist Sas Colby. It was a freeing experience, working first on the paper as a whole, and then dividing it into separate pages. For *Be* I used heavy interfacing, which gives the book a nice weight and made the pages stiff enough to fold.

To punch up the color of the vintage black and white photos, I played with their hue and saturation, then transferred them from transparency to fabric using matte medium. For the diving woman in the layout called "Swim," I applied blue and green oil-pastels to the fabric before doing the transfer.

Be daring, be different, be impractical; be anything that will assert integrity of purpose and imaginative vision against the play-it-safers, the creatures of the commonplace, the slaves of the ordinary.

~ Cecil Beaton

Materials
Craft glue or sewing needle and thread • Craft knife • Embellishments • Fluid acrylic paints • Heavyweight interfacing 24" x 16" • Inkjet transparencies • Iron and ironing board • Matte medium • Paintbrushes • Photos

Method

1. Paint the interfacing with fluid acrylics, watering them down to create soft edges where the colors meet. Let the paint dry and iron the interfacing to set the color.

2. Holding the interfacing by the two short sides, fold it in half from top to bottom, with the painted side out.

3. Fold the interfacing in half again, left to right, and then again, left to right. The interfacing should now be folded to the finished page size. Straighten the edges and burnish the creases using an iron.

4. Open the interfacing. Following Diagrams 1 and 2 in Eight-Fold Books (page 34), cut along the center-line with a craft knife and fold the sections to create the book.

5. Transfer photos onto fabric (see page 21). Glue or stitch the photos and embellishments onto the front cover and pages.

HOME

A boxed portfolio like this can be an excellent group project. For this one, I sent blank pages to eleven other artists with the request that they each create a page on the theme of "home." When all of the pages were returned, I created a fabric-covered, fabric-lined box to hold them.

Home is a name, a word, it is a strong one; stronger than magician ever spoke, or spirit ever answered to, in the strongest conjuration.

~ Charles Dickens

Book

Materials   Manila envelopes for mailing fabric pages • Unstretched canvas or cotton duck

Method

1. Contact the people of your choice and invite them to participate.

2. Cut a 12" x 12" piece of unstretched canvas or cotton duck for each participant.

3. Mail each participant a blank page. Specify the required return date and, if desired, the materials you'd like them to use. Instruct them to work on one side only so the recipient of the portfolio can have a choice of display options.

Box

Materials   Acid-free mat board • Batting, thin or low-loft • Clamps or clothespins • Cording or trim (optional) • Craft glue • Craft knife • Embellishments • Fabric for box cover and lining • Foam core board, ¼" • Large needle • Measuring tape or ruler • Scissors or rotary cutter • Sewing needle (optional) • Straight pins • Thread (optional) • Wire, 20 or 22 gauge • Wire cutters

Method

For twelve, 12" x 12" pages, create a 14" x 14" x 4" box to allow for a lined and padded box interior.

1. Cut the following pieces of foam core for the outer box:

> Two, 14" x 14"
> Two, 14" x 4"
> Two, 13 ¾" x 4"
> Two, 13" x 1"
> Two, 12 ½ x 1"

2. Cut the following pieces of mat board for the box lining:

> One, 13 ½" x 13 ½"
> One, 13 ¾" x 13 ¾"
> Two, 13 ½" x 3 ¾"
> Two, 13 ½" x 3 ¾"

3. Cut the fabric for the box and box lining to the above dimensions plus an extra 1 ½" on all sides for turning and gluing. Exception: For the four 1"-wide strips of foam core, cut the fabric large enough to cover the entire piece.

Susan Shie. Acrylic and marker on canvas. Hand painted.

Karen Michel. Mixed media altered photocollage. Hand stitched and printed.

Sas Colby. Mixed textiles, printed text. Machine stitched.

Lynn Whipple. Mixed media collage. Hand stamped, machine and hand stitched.

4. Pad the bottom and side pieces of foam core with batting. Cut the batting the same size as the foam core. Add glue in a few places to tack it down.

5. Cover all the pieces of foam core with fabric by pulling the fabric to the back of each piece and gluing it in place. Exception: Leave the 1" strips uncovered until after Step 13.

6. To assemble the box, place padded bottom face down, and run a line of glue along two opposite edges of one of 14" x 14" foam core pieces and on the bottom of the two 14" x 4" foam core side pieces. Set the two longer side pieces, padded side out, on the glued areas of the foam core box bottom. Hold the pieces in place by sticking straight pins through the foam core bottom up into the sides. Repeat with two 13 3/4" x 4" side pieces.

7. To line the box, slide the pieces inside the box to ensure that they fit before you cover the mat board with fabric. Mark the two longer side pieces (13 1/2" x 3 3/4") so they can be placed on opposite sides of the box interior. Note: The mat board may appear to fit loosely, but once the fabric and batting are on they should fit snugly. Make sure they are not too tight at this point.

8. Pad the bottom lining board with two or three layers of batting to give it a nice cushion. Cover it with lining fabric.

Patti Culea. Mixed media collage. Machine embroidered.

Claudine Hellmuth. Paper and fabric collage, acrylic paint. Hand painted.

9. Spread glue on the inside of the box bottom and put the bottom lining in place. Weight it with books to ensure good contact.

10. Cover the side pieces with batting and fabric. Place glue on the backs of the side pieces and glue them into place, remembering to put the two longer pieces on the opposite sides of the box interior. Clamp the pieces in place until dry.

Nina Bagley. Image transfer, fabric collage, beading. Hand stitched.

Claire Fenton. Mixed media altered photo collage. Machine embroidered.

Lesley Riley. Image transfer, fabric collage. Machine stitched.

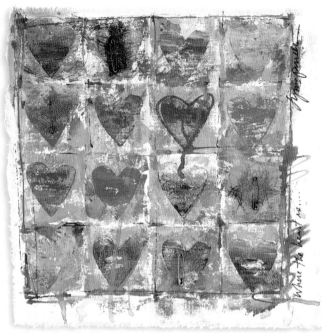

Lynne Perrella. Monoprint, fabric collage. Hand printed.

11. To assemble the box lid, first decorate the lid cover fabric as desired by sewing, fusing, or gluing on fabric collage and embellishments. Pad the foam core box lid with batting. Center the decorated cover fabric over the lid. Pull the fabric around to the back of the lid and glue it in place.

12. Pad one side of the mat board box lid lining and cover it with fabric.

13. Affix the small 1" strips to the box lid lining with wire to prevent the box lid from sliding off. Cut eight 5" pieces of wire. Fold each piece of wire into a U shape and insert two pieces of wire into each strip, 2" from either end. (See Diagram 1).

DIAGRAM 1. U-shaped wires inserted at either end secure 1" strips of fabric-covered foam core to the box lid.

14. Cover both sides of the strips with fabric. Do not pad with batting. Glue the fabric on all sides except where the wire is extending, folding and gluing the fabric around the edges as one would wrap a package.

15. Cut off the excess on the side where the wire extends. Cut a slit with a craft knife so the fabric lies flat around the wire. Smooth and glue the fabric to this edge. *Note: It's OK if it's not perfect—this side of the strip will be hidden.*

16. Center two longer strips on opposite sides of the lid lining, ½" from the outer edge. Mark the spot where the wire meets the lining. Use a large needle to poke a hole into the lid lining and push the wire through the holes. Repeat this for the two shorter sides, fitting them between the longer sides ½" from the outer edge. (See Diagram 2.)

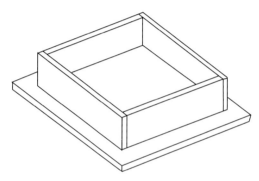

DIAGRAM 2. The shorter sides of the box lid fit snugly between the ends of the longer sides.

17. Before securing the wire, run a line of glue along the edge of each strip where it meets the box lid lining and at the corners where the strips meet. Pull the wire snugly towards the back of the board and twist it to hold the strips in place. Add straight pins to hold the corners in place until they dry. Trim the excess and press the ends flat against the lid lining.

18. Glue the lid lining to the lid cover. As a decorative option, insert cording or trim between the two layers before adhering them together.

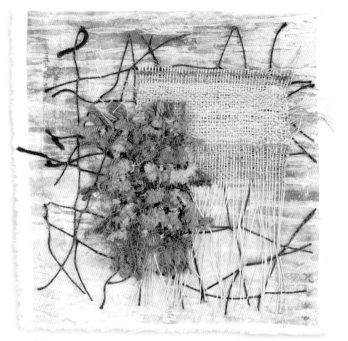

Mary Fisher. Acrylics and hand-woven textiles. Hand stitched

Laura Wasilowski. Fused cotton on canvas. Machine quilted.

Accordion-Folded Books

The projects in this section all rely on one basic book construction technique—an accordion-folded binding. Such books can be made from one single piece of fabric folded accordion—style, or from single pages hinged with fabric to create an accordion-fold. While the concept behind the binding is simple enough, accordion-folded projects can range from the refreshingly simple to the deliciously complex.

Single-Page Accordion Books

For single-page construction, first determine the number and size of the pages you want in your book. Multiply the page width by the number of pages and cut a length of fabric or interfacing that length by the desired page height. For example, a book with eight 4"-wide and 6"-tall pages requires a piece of fabric or interfacing 32" wide and 6" tall (4" x 8" = 32"). To fold your finished length into a book, measure one page width and create a fold. Fold the fabric or interfacing back and forth, dividing the fabric evenly between the pages.

Separate-Page Accordion Books

To hinge separate pages together for an accordion fold, cut strips of fabric as tall as each page and 1" wide. Lay out the pages in the desired order. Starting on the right side of the cover page, stitch one side of a strip to the back of each page edge with a 1/4" seam. The extra 1/2" of fabric between the stitched edges allows for the folding of the book.

Accordion-folded bindings can be as simple or elaborate as your design.

Reinforcing Pages for Better Accordion Folds

Whether you use a single page or separate pages for your accordion-fold books, you may need to reinforce your fabric with interfacing so it's sturdy enough to hold a crisp fold. To do this, cut two pieces of fabric the desired length and height plus one inch (7" x 33" for a 6" x 32" finished piece). Then cut a piece of medium to heavyweight interfacing the size of the finished piece plus ¼". Pin both fabrics together, right-sides-together, and lay the interfacing on top. Stitch a ½" seam around all four sides, leaving a 4" opening on one side to turn the piece right side out. After turning the piece, hand-stitch the opening closed, iron the fabric smooth, then fold it accordion style and iron to set the folds. An alternative to this approach is to stitch the fabrics together with the wrong sides together and the interfacing sandwiched between. Sew all four sides of the fabric and leave the edges unfinished.

Star-Folded Books

A star-folded book is made the same way as an accordion-folded book, but the first and last pages of the accordion are joined together and the book is folded to create a star. As a result, there is no first page, last page, or cover. Whether you choose the single-page or separate-page approach to creating the accordion for this book, keep in mind that you will collage on one side of the fabric only, as the back will be bound in place.

To determine the number of pages that you'll create for your star-folded book, double the number of points you want the star to have. For instance, a six-pointed star such as *Starbook* (page 60) will have twelve pages. To determine the length of your base

fabric when using the single-page approach, select a page width and multiply it by the number of pages (in this case, twelve). For example, a page 5" wide requires a length of fabric that is 60" long. Add a 1" seam allowance if you plan to finish the edges and turn it inside out.

Use chalk or pins to mark where each page will folded, then sew, glue or fuse photos, fabric, and ephemera to each page, being mindful of the fold lines. If you have added a seam allowance to your length of fabric, be sure you do not add anything that will interfere with sewing those seams, especially if you will be machine stitching. Wait to add anything that may interfere with sewing and turning until after you have completed those steps. If you are creating a book with finished seams, complete your page design, then place the fabric face down onto the front side of your backing fabric. Place the interfacing on top and pin all the layers together. Stitch around all four edges, leaving an opening to turn the piece right side out. Turn and iron. Stitch down each page edge through all the layers to hold them together.

To finish, hand-stitch the two ends of the fabric strip together to form a ring, with the artwork facing outward. Fold the fabric along each page edge to create a star shape and iron to set the folds. Pinch and pin the inner folds together and hand stitch them in place to hold the star shape. (See Diagram 1.)

DIAGRAM 1. Pin then sew the inner folds of the star as indicated by the dashed lines of this diagram.

ITALY 2003

I was watching the movie *The Affair of the Necklace* while gathering fabrics for this book. Even though the movie was set in France and my book depicts my daughter in Italy, the period costumes and scenery inspired my design. Canvas panels make an ideal base for this project because they are inexpensive, readily available, and sturdy enough to hold relatively heavy three-dimensional objects.

To give a book containing recent photos an Old World feel, combine richly textured brocades with different color ribbons and images from classical art. Unite the various layouts with a common element, such as a certain shade of red and just a touch of white.

You may have the universe if I may have Italy.

~ Giuseppe Verdi

Materials Clamps • Ephemera and embellishments • Fabric to cover boards and for collage • Fabric glue • Fringe (optional) • Inkjet-ready fabric • Photos • Photo paper • Ribbon, 1" wide • Scissors or rotary cutter • Ten canvas boards, 5" x 7"

Method

1. To create smooth edges on the canvas boards, trim the jagged corner area where the canvas is folded over. Cover the boards with fabric using fabric glue.

2. Print photos onto inkjet-ready fabric and photo paper.

3. Create your fabric and photo collages for each panel, glue them in place, and embellish as desired. *Note: Leave one panel free of collage and embellishment to use as the outside back cover.*

4. Create the front cover by decorating one side of one panel to reflect the theme of the book.

Italy 2003

a little shopping in Florence

La Frateria

Convento di San Francesco

Cetona, Siena

4. Place the top row of panels, art-side down, and the bottom row, art-side up, with ¼" of space between each panel. (See Diagram 1.) Note: If a panel will have embellishment with a high profile, allow more than ¼" between that panel and the one it folds onto.

FACE DOWN

| FRONT COVER | | | | INSIDE BACK COVER |
| INSIDE FRONT COVER | | | | BACK COVER |

FACE UP

DIAGRAM 1. For an accordion-folded book with double-sided pages, place one row of pages art-side down above one row of pages art-side up.

5. Glue one piece of ribbon across all of the panels on the top row, 1 ½" from the top of the panels. Glue a second piece across all the panels on the top row starting 1 ½" from the bottom of the panels.

6. Spread glue across the backs of the top row of panels. Place each panel from the bottom row on top of the panel directly above it. Clamp or weight the panels until the glue dries. *Note: To add fringe between panels, glue it into position before gluing the two rows of panels together. Keep in mind that embellished edges are best on the end panel to avoid interfering with the accordion folds.*

7. Fold the book into position, or display it standing in a zigzag placement.

SEW WHAT

Sew What is a sampler book of different materials and techniques you can use in making fabric books. It includes heavy watercolor paper, copper mesh, brown paper bags, transparencies, mica, and more. The contrasting textures make the book a more interesting tactile and visual experience.

In fabric memory books, the idea is to fashion pages that are as tantalizing to the fingertips as they are to the eyes. Combine hard and soft textures, paper, paint, and pictures to create something enigmatic and unique.

Those who danced were thought to be quite insane by those who could not hear the music.

~ Angela Monet

Materials

140-lb watercolor paper • Brown paper bag • Burnisher • Copper sheeting, lightweight • Fabric scraps • Fine copper mesh • Fluid acrylics • Heavy-duty thread • Images • Inkjet-ready fabric • Iron and ironing board • Metallic craft paint • Mica • Paintbrushes • Press cloth • Scissors • Sewing machine • Soft gel medium • Spun-bonded paper • Stencil • Tongs and butane torch (optional) • Transparencies

Method

1. Prepare the images. Print some of them on inkjet-ready fabric, some on transparencies. (See page 20.)

2. Cut four pieces of watercolor paper the desired page size. Paint them with fluid acrylics and metallic paint, letting the layers of paint dry between applications for optimal color. When dry, spread soft gel medium on the pages to seal them. *Note: One page for this book has a copper mesh, rather than a paper, base.*

3. Create a collage for each page using fabric, images, and other materials. The techniques I used to create the different pages of my book include the following:

A. Stencil a design on the page using metallic paint. Create a collage by stitching a piece of fabric and a transparency photo over copper sheeting. Sew the collage to the page. If desired, use tongs to hold the copper sheeting in a flame to give it a patina before you sew with it.

Accordion books lend themselves
easily to a variety of display options.

B. Create a page from fine copper mesh by cutting it to be 1 $\frac{1}{2}$" larger on all sides than the finished page size. If desired, use tongs to hold the copper mesh in a flame to give it a patina. Fold the raw edges of the mesh in twice, first $\frac{1}{2}$", then 1". Miter the corners, trimming the excess mesh. Stitch fabric and a photo printed on fabric to the copper mesh.

C. Cut a piece of spun-bonded paper large enough to frame the desired image and paint it with metallic paint. Transfer the image from transparency to the spun-bonded paper using soft gel medium and a burnisher (see page 21). Working in a well-ventilated area, cover the transferred image with a block or a book and, using a press cloth, iron the edges of the spun-bonded paper.

D. Cover four small images printed on fabric with four rectangles of mica. Stitch the mica-covered

images in place. (See Book Smarts, page 113.)

E. Cut a piece of fabric large enough to cover a watercolor paper page. Stitch it into place. Cut a paper bag slightly larger than the desired image and paint it with metallic paint. Transfer the image from a transparency onto the paper bag using soft gel medium. Cut a second transparency of the same image in half and stitch the transparency over the corresponding half that you transferred to the bag. Stitch the bag to the page.

4. To bind the pages together, cut strips of fabric 1" wide and the height of the book page. Lay out the pages in order. Starting on the right side of the cover page, stitch one side of the fabric strip to the back of each page edge with a $\frac{1}{4}$" seam, leaving $\frac{1}{2}$" of the fabric strip free between the pages to allow the book to fold.

BOOK smarts

Because an accordion book begs to be stretched out and viewed all at once, it's more important than ever to pay attention to how the composition of each page works with the other pages. One strategy is to create unity between the pages by using similar colors and textures while creating interest by alternating layout patterns and details such as which direction people in photos face.

THE RAINY DAY

To many, destroying an old book is a sacrilege, but isn't it better to make something beautiful and loved out of something old and forgotten? The cover used for *Rainy Day* was from an older book whose interior pages were almost completely detached from the spine. After removing the pages, I reinforced the spine and gave it new pages made from an accordion-folded length of interfacing.

I adhered decorative ribbons to the inside covers under the book lining to create a way to keep the book closed (and its secrets hidden) for a rainy day.

Life is like a rainbow. You need both the sun and the rain to make its colors appear.

~ Unknown

Materials

Clamps · **Fabric for book lining** · **Fabric for spine reinforcement** · **Fabric glue** · **Fluid acrylic paints** · **Iron and ironing board** · **Iron-on fusible** · **Measuring tape or ruler** · **Medium-weight interfacing** · **Old book** · **Paintbrushes** · **Permanent pen** · **Ribbon** · **Scissors or rotary cutter**

Method

1. Remove the stack of pages from the book. Measure the height and width of a page to determine your new page size.

2. Glue fabric to both the inside and outside of the spine to reinforce and decorate it.

3. Measure the inside of the book and cut the lining fabric to size, plus 1" all around. Cut a piece of interfacing slightly smaller than the inside cover and, using iron-on fusible, fuse it to fabric. Fold the excess fabric over to the back of the interfacing and iron it in place.

4. Glue the book lining to the inside of the book cover, inserting the ends of the ribbons under the outer edges if so desired. Clamp the lining in place until it dries.

5. Multiply the desired number of pages by the page width and height as determined in step 1. Cut a length of interfacing to these dimensions.

6. Paint the interfacing with fluid acrylics. Let it dry, then fold the interfacing, accordion-style, into pages.

7. Center the bottom page onto the inside back cover and glue it in place, making sure the pages will open outward and to the right.

8. Write cherished secrets inside.

STARBOOK

What stellar person or memory in your life deserves to be the focus of your Starbook? I had just finished a quilt using these images of my mother and decided to reduce them and create a star-fold book to accompany the quilt. Each collage was machine stitched, with the safety pins added for fun.

Though my soul may set in darkness, it will rise in perfect light. I have loved the stars too fondly to be fearful of the night.

~ Sarah Williams

Materials

Beads • Copper wire, 22 gauge • Cording • Fabric long enough for front and back of book • Fabric for collage • Heavy-duty thread • Inkjet-ready fabric • Iron and ironing board • Iron-on fusible (optional) • Measuring tape or ruler • Medium or heavyweight interfacing • Photos printed • Safety pins • Scissors or rotary cutter • Sewing needle • Straight pins

Method

1. Select a fabric for the front and back of the pages and cut each to size plus the margins. (See Star-Folded Books, page 49.) Reinforce with interfacing if necessary, cutting it to the size of the fabric plus ¼".

2. Temporarily mark the page margins on the front fabric with pins to avoid working into the seam allowances or other pages.

3. Create the fabric and photo collage for each page and stitch or fuse each one in place.

4. Stitch together the front and the back, art-side-in, leaving an opening for turning the fabric. Turn the fabric, iron to set the seams, and hand-sew the two ends of the book together with the artwork facing outward.

5. Fold the book into a star and pin or stitch it to hold the shape.

6. To create the wire embellishment, insert wire into three lengths of cording. Bend one end of each wire and gather the cording along it. On the opposite end of the wire, add beads and bend the wire back into the last bead.

7. Insert the wired cords into the center of the book between the pinned folds.

8. Using strong thread, stitch the inside folds together to hold the star shape.

9. Add safety pins for a decorative element.

Button-Bound and Button-Jointed Books

Buttons and fabric memory books are a natural match. Not only are buttons appealing design elements, they also can be a key part of a durable binding by preventing stitches from pulling through layers of fabric. The projects in this chapter include several that use one of my all-time favorite techniques—button binding—plus one that puts a playful spin on standard book bindings with a button-jointed binding that allows pages to swivel open and closed.

Button Bindings

A button binding works equally well with separate pages and signatures, and it can accommodate a single piece of cover material that folds over all the pages or separate cover pages that go on the top and bottom of your stack. To create a button binding, place one button on the front cover and another behind it on the back cover, line up your covers and pages, and sew through the layers to connect the two buttons. Sew a row of buttons along the spine to complete the binding.

To spice up the cover of a button-bound book, mix the colors and sizes of the buttons.

A black button connects a page with photos of a young girl to a page with black polka dots in this button-jointed book.

Button-Jointed Bindings

A button-jointed binding connects a stack of pages with a series of buttons and buttonholes. For instance, by placing a button on the right side of a page, and a buttonhole on the left, you can create a book in which the pages swivel out for viewing and swivel back to close, as in *Round & Round* (page 76).

If you add buttons and buttonholes to each page with the artwork facing you in the correct orientation, when you open the book so the pages are in a straight line, every other page will be upside-down. If you want all of the pages to open right side up, flip every other page upside-down before you add the buttons and buttonholes.

BERRY CHERRY

This is the first fabric book I made. The interesting thing is, all of the methods used in this book serve me well today. For instance, I tea-dyed many of the newer fabrics to blend in with vintage, and backed them all with iron-on fusible so that the only sewing I needed to do was for the button binding.

There is a garden in her face,
Where roses and white lilies show;
A heavenly paradise is that place,
Wherein all pleasant fruits do grow.
There cherries hang that none may buy,
Till cherry ripe themselves do cry.

Unknown

I had wanted to make a fabric book for years, but never knew where to start. One day, I just jumped in and figured it out as I went along. This book was the result.

One must ask children and birds how cherries and strawberries taste.

~ Goethe

Materials

Assorted fabrics, including vintage napkins, dishtowels, and laces • Buttons for binding • Coffee or tea (optional) • Clamps • Heavy-duty thread for binding • Inkjet-ready fabric • Iron and ironing board • Iron-on fusible • Photos printed • Quotes • Scissors or rotary cutter • Sewing needle

Method

1. Gather assorted fabrics. Soak new fabrics in prepared coffee or tea if a vintage look is desired.

2. Back the fabrics with iron-on fusible and cut some to page size. *Note: This design calls for an even number of pages.*

3. Print photos and quotes onto inkjet-ready fabric (see page 20). Using iron-on fusible, back the printed photos and quotes. Cut out the photos and quotes.

4. Create a collage on each page, adding photos, quotes, lace, fabric snippets, etc., leaving a 1" margin on the binding side.

Can she bake a cherry pie,
Billy Boy, Billy Boy?
Can she bake a cherry pie,
Charming Billy?
She can bake a cherry pie,
Quick's a cat can wink her eye.
She's a young thing,
And cannot leave her mother.

5. Place two pages back-to-back and iron them to fuse the pages and their collages. Repeat this for the remaining pages.

6. Stack the pages and determine the size of the cover. *Note: The front and back covers will be formed by a single piece of fabric that wraps around the side of the stack.*

7. Decorate the cover.

8. Using iron-on fusible, iron the inside cover fabric onto the back of the decorated cover.

9. Place the cover over the page stack, making sure the pages are snug against the inside cover. Clamp the book to hold the pieces in place.

10. To bind, see Button Bindings, page 62. Space the buttons evenly, beginning about one inch from the top and bottom.

STONE ANGELS

Darlene Troyer captures the soul that is in stone, photographing cemetery statuary all over the country. When she offered me images to use in my art, I jumped at the chance. The original photographs are beautiful, but I couldn't resist increasing the saturation by 100 percent to get a more radiant color for this button-bound project.

This project showed me that there can be a rich range of color in stone. To complement the images, I chose a palette of blue, green, and pink fabrics along with quotes from my collection.

Even empty spaces and silence can be the wings and voices of angels.

~ Michele Linfante

Materials

Assorted fabrics for pages and collage • Clamps • Inkjet-ready fabric • Iron and ironing board • Iron-on fusible • Photos • Quotes • Scissors or rotary cutter • Sewing needle • Six buttons or more • Two large pieces of fabric • Thread

Method

1. Print photos and quotes onto inkjet-ready fabric (see page 20). Back them with iron-on fusible before cutting them out to prevent the edges from fraying.

2. Cut the fabric to the desired page size. Create an even number of pages.

3. Working on single pages, create a collage on each page, leaving a 1" margin on the binding side. Fuse or stitch the designs in place.

4. Place two pages back-to-back; fuse or stitch them together around all four edges.

5. Stack the pages and determine the size of the covers. *Note: The front and back covers will be formed by a single piece of fabric that wraps around the side of the stack.*

6. Cut the cover and the inside-cover fabric to size and, with the backs together, fuse or stitch them in place.

7. Fold the cover over the page stack, making sure the pages are snug against the cover fold. Clamp everything in place to hold.

8. To bind, see Button Bindings, page 62. Space the buttons evenly, beginning about one inch from the top and bottom.

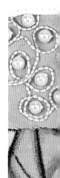

angel in
until I s
Michaelange

What you leave behind is not what
is engraved in stone monuments,
but what is woven into the
lives of others.

Pericles

BOOK smarts

When creating a wraparound cover for a button-bound book, allow for a slight overlap at the top, bottom, and right edges, plus an allowance to make a spine appropriate for the thickness of the pages.

FABRIC JOURNAL

Like most people who love fabric, I find that actually cutting and using it can be difficult because once it's gone, it's gone. Finally, it dawned on me to create a fabric journal where I can hoard those last precious bits of favorite fabrics. Not only does this book hold memories of projects past, it reminds me there's always another beautiful fabric waiting to be found.

Though for me the pleasure of this memory book lies in the visual and tactile reminders it holds, other people seem to find it interesting for the variety of samples contains.

Memory is a crazy woman that hoards colored rags and throws away food.

~ Austin O'Malley

Materials

Buttons • Computer and inkjet printer • Fabric • Inkjet-ready fabric • Iron and ironing board • Iron-on fusible • Scissors or rotary cutter • Sewing needle (optional) • Sheer fabric for pages • Small swatches of your favorite fabrics • Thread (optional)

Method

1. Collect fabric scraps and cut them into similar sizes.

2. Determine the book size and how many swatches will be on each page. Allow a 1" margin on the left side for the binding.

3. Stitch or fuse each swatch to the page in a grid format, leaving room for labels.

4. Take your sewn swatch pages to the computer and type up a sheet of labels, leaving enough space between each label for cutting.

5. Print the labels on inkjet-ready fabric. Back the fabric with iron-on fusible, if desired.

6. Cut out the labels and fuse or stitch them under the fabric swatches.

7. Stack the completed pages together and determine the cover size.

8. Decorate the front cover. Fuse or stitch the inside cover fabric to the outside cover fabric.

9. Insert the page stack. To bind, sew from the top to attach the top button, stitch through all the layers and through the button on the back cover. Repeat for each button.

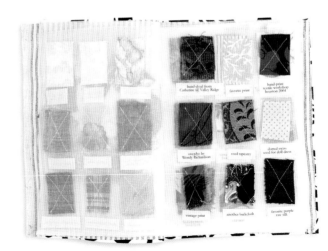

NATURAL RESOURCES

Who can resist vintage textiles and their history? When I hold a piece of material that another woman wore or used in her home a hundred years ago, I try to imagine the lives that became woven into it. I wanted to create a book in which vintage textiles were the focus, so I chose a design similar to a fabric sample book to accommodate items of different sizes. A backing board provides the necessary support for these delicate possessions.

Natural Resources

Words didn't seem necessary for this fabric memory book, but when I came across one of my favorite poems, "Natural Resources" by Adrienne Rich, I added it to the back page and named the project for it.

No person who can read is ever successful at cleaning out an attic.

~Ann Landers

Materials

Acid-free mat board • Balsa wood, 1" strip as long as the widest textile • Clamps • Craft knife • Fabric (first-aid) tape or duct tape • Fabric glue • Fabric • Five or six large buttons • Heavy-duty thread • Inkjet-ready fabric • Iron and ironing board • Iron-on fusible • Large needle • Measuring tape or ruler • Muslin • Photos • Scissors or rotary cutter • Vintage textiles (handkerchiefs, dish or hand towels, doilies, etc.)

Method

1. Choose several vintage textiles and stack them according to size, with the largest on the bottom.

2. Align them at the top edge. Reinforce the top edge of delicate vintage textiles by applying a 1" strip of iron-on fusible or by folding a 2" piece of muslin over the top edge.

3. Measure the width and length of the largest vintage textile. Cut two pieces of mat board the size of the largest vintage textile plus ¼" all around.

4. Spread a thin layer of fabric glue on one side of one mat board and cover it with the fabric. Fold and glue the fabric edges on the back. Do not cover the second mat board at this time. *Note: The fabric will show behind the last vintage textile.*

5. Cut the balsa wood into a strip as wide as the largest vintage textile minus $\frac{1}{2}$". If you will not cover the strip by folding over a vintage textile, cover it with muslin to hide it.

6. Print photos onto inkjet-ready fabric (see page 20). Apply iron-on fusible to the back of the photos. Trim the images to size and iron them to each vintage textile. Add hand or machine stitching if desired.

7. Place all but the top (cover) textile on the backing board in the intended order. If desired, fold over the vintage textile on the bottom to cover the reinforcement strip. If not, put the reinforcement strip in place $\frac{1}{4}$" from the top of the backing board. Cover the strip with the top vintage textile. Clamp the top edge to hold everything in place.

8. Determine the location for the buttons, spacing them evenly across the top and starting about 1" from the side edge. Using a large needle, make a hole through each buttonhole and the rein-forcement strip, textile layers, and backing board.

9. To bind, start from the back. Leaving a 6" thread tail, sew up through all the layers, the top button, and back down. Leave another 6" thread tail. Tie the two threads together with two or three knots.

10. Add glue to one side of the second backing board and cover it with fabric, folding and gluing the edges around the back.

11. Glue the backs of the backing boards together.

ROUND & ROUND

One day, I was talking with my friend Christine about our circle of friends, and we decided to create a book for a particularly generous member of this group. Thinking of friendship, we brainstormed the idea for a jointed circle. To help the circle theme shine through, I chose graduated circles of polka-dotted fabric, round buttons, and a limited color palette.

This button-jointed binding is a fun technique that works best with relatively stiff material. To stiffen the lighter weight fabrics I wanted for *Round and Round* I constructed each circular page from two pieces of fabric, one piece of heavyweight interfacing, and two pieces of iron-on fusible.

A circle is a necessity. Otherwise you would see no one. We each have our circle.

~ Gertrude Stein

Materials

Buttons • Craft knife • Heavyweight interfacing, 1/2 yard • Inkjet-ready fabric • Iron and ironing board • Iron-on fusible • Pencil • Photos • Scraps of fabric • Seven circle templates in various sizes • Sewing machine • Sewing needle • Thread

Method

1. Determine which fabrics to use for each size circle. Back the two fabric pieces for each circle with iron-on fusible over an area slightly larger than the size of the circle before cutting.

2. Trace one circle template onto the front of two pieces of fusible-backed fabric and one piece of heavyweight interfacing. Repeat for each of the other six sizes of circle templates.

3. Print photos onto inkjet-ready fabric (see page 20). Create a fabric and photo collage on the front of each page (the back is optional) and sew or fuse the collage in place.

4. Iron to fuse the front and back fabrics to the heavyweight interfacing circles.

5. Machine zigzag ⅛" from the outer edge of the circle using a wide zigzag stitch and a .5mm stitch length with a coordinating or contrasting thread. *Note: To achieve the best look, match the bobbin with the top thread.*

6. Trim the edges just to the zigzag stitch.

7. On the bottom (largest) page, sew a button to the right side of the circle.

8. Take the next smaller page and center it on top of the page underneath to determine the buttonhole position.
Using straight pins, find the edges of the button underneath and mark the top fabric where the buttonhole should be placed.

9. Using a craft knife, slash a buttonhole through all the layers. Check to see that the button fits through the hole; lengthen it if needed.

BOOK
smarts
Head for the kitchen when you need perfectly round templates of varying sizes. Lay plates, bowls, cans, cups, glasses, pots, etc. on your fabric and trace around the outside with a pencil. Cut carefully along the lines and you have a perfect circle.

10. To face the buttonhole, cut two rectangles from the same or a coordinating fabric that has been backed with iron-on fusible. The rectangles should be slightly smaller than the length of the buttonhole and $\frac{1}{4}"$ to $\frac{1}{2}"$ wide. Fold over one rectangle on each side of the buttonhole and iron to fuse them in place.

11. Repeat steps 7–10 on each page, sewing a button onto one side of the circle and making a buttonhole on the other side of the circle that fits the button on the page beneath.

12. Button the pages together and enjoy.

Sewn-Binding Books

Stitched by hand or by machine, sewn bindings are a classic choice for a fabric memory book. They can be as easy to plan and execute as stacking loose pages and sewing along the left edge, as in a simple sewn binding; unusual as stitching separate pages to a strip of cloth or ribbon for a staggered-layer binding; or as sophisticated as sewing signature-constructed pages.

Simple Sewn Bindings

A simple sewn binding is just that—a stack of pages stitched together along the left edge. It's an excellent choice if you're just getting started with sewn bindings or if you want your design to feel spontaneous, as I did with the book *Finds* (page 82). With this type of binding you can add separate front and back covers to the stack or fold one piece of fabric over the stack to create a cover. If your book is too thick to fit under your sewing machine foot, hand-stitch the binding.

Staggered-Layer Bindings

To create a staggered-layer binding, sew each page to a strip of material adjacent to, not on top of, the page before it, so that when the binding is laid flat the pages appear to be staggered. You can play with this effect further by using pages with uneven edges, as I did with *The New Star* (page 88).

Sometimes the best way to bind a book is the straightforward approach of a simple sewn binding that will not compete for attention against other design elements.

For a staggered-layer binding, sew each page separately to a strip of fabric or length of ribbon.

Start with a material (fabric, ribbon, leather, etc.) that is wide enough for each page to be stitched to it separately. Sew the bottom page or back cover of the book on the right-hand side of the binding fabric. Then sew the next page about ¼" to the left of the first page. Repeat until all pages have been sewn to the binding fabric. If you start with a piece of fabric that's too wide, you can trim the excess when you finish binding all the pages, or flip the excess over the front page and create a nice finished edge.

Sewn-Signature Books

Many book artists use complicated techniques for sewing signatures. I prefer a simple approach in which you sew two stitches and tie the thread either in the center of the signature fold or on the outside of the spine. Depending on the size of the book, you can take one or several stitches down the length of the centerline.

To use this method to attach a stack of signatures to a cover, assemble an unsewn signature and fold it along the center. Stack the signatures and fold the cover over the stack, lining up the parts of the book. Be sure that the cover has enough fabric to allow for the depth of the signatures while also extending about ¼" over the right top and right bottom edges of the signature stack. Open to the center of each signature and mark the location where you will place your stitches by pushing a straight pin through the center seam and out the cover on the spine.

The number of stitches you make will depend on the size of the book and your design. Most likely, you will want to line up your stitches to create a uniform appearance along the spine. Virtually any thread-like substance that fits through the eye of a needle will make a good signature binding-just keep in mind that delicate fabrics may be damaged by heavier threads, and heavy fabrics may break delicate bindings. A few you may want to try include embroidery floss, beading thread, pearl cotton, ribbon, twine, upholstery thread, and yarn.

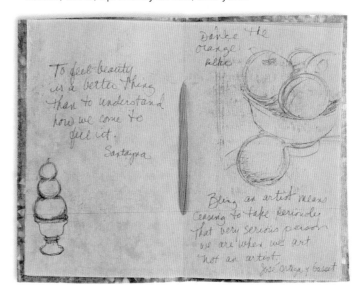

One large stitch down the centerline of this spread holds the signature together and binds it to the cover. The loose ends of the stitch are tied on the outside of the book's spine, adding a decorative element to the cover of *Chapbook* (page 94).

FINDS

Finds is a book created from things I discovered at a vintage textile show. Almost everything there was too expensive, but I dug out a few wonderful scraps—leftovers from other people's projects that still had untapped potential waiting to be unleashed. To retain the spontaneous energy of the scraps, I did as little cutting and sewing as possible, and chose a simple sewn binding.

If you need creative inspiration, limit yourself to four or five fabrics and create a simple book. You may find yourself being more inventive and daring when you don't have your usual range of supplies to rescue you.

Those who don't believe in magic will never find it.

~ Roald Dahl

Materials
Fabric and paper remnants and scraps • **Needle** • **Sewing machine (optional)** • **Thread** • **Vintage buttons** • **Vintage trim**

Method

1. Create pages from the fabric scraps. They do not all have to be the same size.

2. Collage and embellish each page with the fabrics, trims, and buttons.

3. Choose a cover fabric and embellish it.

4. Stack the finished pages and place the cover over them.

5. Hand or machine stitch down the left edge of all layers to bind the book.

6. Cut several strips of fabric about ½" wide. Knot each end and tie it in a loose knot in the center. Stitch the strips down along the bound edge to embellish.

BIRDS OF A FEATHER

Feathering the nest, an empty nest, the nesting instinct—like a magpie, I gathered the materials for this book, not knowing quite what it would look like. I collected dyed silk cocoons that look like eggs, vintage bird prints, yarn that mimics a nest… but still, I was missing a vision. A feather trim found in a craft store made it all come clear. I couldn't wait to start.

This fabric memory book has a rigid back that helps protect the feather trim from breakage when the book is handled. Hand-dyed silk ribbon added to the sewn-signature binding is another unusual element.

Use what talents you possess: the wood would be very silent if no birds sang there except those that sang best.

~ Henry Van Dyke

Materials

Acid-free mat board • Batting • Burnisher • Clamps • Cover image • Craft knife • Crewel needle • Fabrics • Fabric glue • Feather trim • Fine-mist spray bottle • Glossy photo paper • Matte medium • Measuring tape or ruler • Pencil • Scissors or rotary cutter • Straight pins • Text and images • Thread • Transparencies

Method

1. To create a book with twenty-four 7 ½ x 9" double-sided pages, cut or tear fabric into twelve double-wide (14" x 9") pieces. (See Signature Construction, page 30). *Note: The finished book will have 24 pages.*

2. Reverse-print the text and images onto transparencies and the cover image on glossy photo paper. Transfer the images and text onto each fabric page and create collages (see page 21). *Note: As you collage your pages, remember to pay attention to your final layout. See page 30 for tips.*

3. Pair collaged double-wide pages and stitch or fuse them back-to-back to create double-sided pages. Arrange the pages into two signatures with twelve 7 ½ x 9" double-sided pages each.

4. Stack the finished signatures together and determine the size for the fabric cover, allowing for enough fabric to cover the top and side of book, plus 4".

5. Transfer the cover image and create the cover design and artwork.

6. Cut one 8" x 9" piece of mat board for the bookboard and one 8 1/2" X 9 1/2" piece of mat board for the backboard. Cut fabric to cover one side of each board, plus 1" on all sides.

7. Cover one side of each board with batting. Center each board, batting-side down, on the back of the fabric. Fold and glue the edges of the fabric to the back of the board.

8. Put the backboard (the larger board) fabric side down on a flat surface. Glue the feather trim around all four edges, placing the tape edge 1/4" from the board edge. Secure the trim with clamps and let it dry.

9. Wrap the cover fabric over the signature stack to determine where to sew the signatures. With the cover fabric in place over closed and stacked signatures, slightly open one signature at a time and stick a straight pin from the center of the signature spread out through the spine at evenly spaced intervals. Mark the locations of the pins on the outside of the cover fabric and inside the center spreads with pencil dots so you will know where to stitch.

10. Open a spread and, aiming towards the pencil dot on the spine, make a stitch through all the pages of the signature, leaving a 5" to 6" tail. Stitch back out through the signatures and spine, creating a 1" to 2" stitch and leaving a tail. Tie the tails together and knot them securely. Repeat down the length of the signature. Repeat for the second signature.

11. Place the backboard fabric side down, spread glue across its back, and place the 4" piece of cover fabric over the glue.

12. Place the book board, fabric side up, on top of the cover material and backboard, sandwiching the cover material and securing the book. Weight the boards until they are dry.

13. Add decorative ribbon to the threads of the outer binding on the cover.

The book-board, here covered with a patterned fabric, is attached to the feathered backboard.

THE NEW STAR

Layering sheer fabrics can produce rich, painterly hues. For best results, aim for fabrics from the same side of the color wheel and pay attention to the cumulative effect of shapes, textures, and colors as the pages come together. For each page of this book, I layered images, text, and sheer fabrics between two pieces of tulle, then stagger bound the pages onto a wired ribbon.

The star of this fabric memory book is my friend's mother, Virginia Glenn Haussler. Ginni painted and wrote poetry and penned "The New Star" while in high school. When I read it, I knew it was the perfect text for this book.

Poetry is a speaking picture.

~ Simonides

Materials

A selection of sheer fabrics • Iron and ironing board • Iron-on fusible • Inkjet-ready fabric, adhesive-backed and plain • Photos • Scissors or rotary cutter • Sewing needle • Straight pins • Text • Thread • Tulle • Wired ribbon (2 ½" wide for a six-page book)

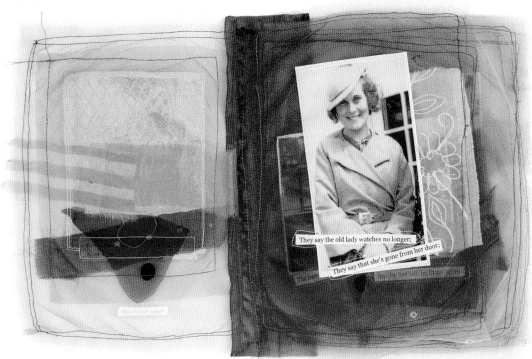

Method

1. Print photos onto adhesive-backed inkjet-ready fabric (see page 20). Cut out the photos, leaving the paper backing in place.

2. Print text onto plain inkjet-ready fabric. Back the fabric with iron-on fusible. Cut out the text.

3. Cut two pieces of tulle to the desired page size. Arrange a photo and sheer fabrics onto one piece of tulle. When you like the collage, remove the paper from the adhesive-backed photo and apply it to the tulle. *Note: The adhesive on the back of the photo print will hold down the other elements of the collage. It may also stick slightly to the surface beneath it, but unless the surface is paper, this shouldn't cause any problems.*

4. Cover the collaged layer with another tulle page and pin them together. Using a low setting appropriate for synthetics, iron the pages to tack down the small text pieces. Stitch around the photo and text to encase them in the tulle. Stitch around all four edges of the pages two or three times to hold the tulle layers in place and define the edges.

BOOK smarts

Working with sheers is a sheer delight—if you know how to tame them. For instance, there is an adhesive-backed, inkjet-ready fabric that makes collaging with sheers easier by holding them in place. To create regular shapes and even-edged pages with a fabric such as tulle, iron it to freezer paper before cutting.

The candlelight bright has ceased its burning

And by her will be lit no more.

5. Repeat steps 3 and 4 to create more pages.

6. Cut a length of ribbon slightly longer than the biggest page plus 1". Fold the two ends of the ribbon in to create a spine for the book slightly longer the biggest page. Hem the fold of the ribbon on both ends.

7. Beginning with the last page, align it on the right side of the ribbon. Pin it in place and stitch the edge of the page to the ribbon.

8. Count the pages and figure out how to space them on the ribbon. Pin the next page to the ribbon at the calculated spacing and stitch it in place. Repeat this step with each page. Stitch the cover along the left margin of the ribbon.

Up in the sky I see a new star shining,

A celestial being burning ever bright.

HOOKED ON BOOKS

Once upon a time, I tried latch hooking a rug. I lost interest before I got very far—all those pieces of yarn! Years later, I came across my latch hook and thought to try it with fabric strips. This time, I loved the color and texture that grew inch by inch. When I was done, I thought the results would make such a welcoming cover that *The Guest Book* was born.

Though latch hooking the cover of this sewn-signature book took me longer than I thought it would, it was a pleasure to work with the colorful fabric scraps. The project was nicely portable too—I traveled with a baggie full of fabric strips, the latch hook, and a canvas so I could make the most of free moments.

Materials

Assorted fabric scraps • Fabric • Fluid acrylic paints • Heavy-duty thread • Interfacing, heavyweight and lightweight • Iron and ironing board • Iron-on fusible • Latch hook • Latch hook rug canvas, 4 squares/inch • Measuring tape or ruler • Paintbrushes • Scissors or rotary cutter • Sewing needle

Method

1. Determine the finished size of your book cover. Cut a piece of latch hook rug canvas that is as tall and twice as wide as the finished size plus 1" all around. (For example, to create a book that is 4 ½" x 6", I began with a canvas that was 10" x 7".)

2. Cut 864 (24 x 36 = 864) assorted fabric strips approximately ½" x 5". Cut on the bias (diagonal) to prevent the fabric from fraying. *Note: A rotary cutter is a great way to cut strips quickly.*

3. Leaving a ½" border on all sides, hook the fabric strips in a random color pattern until the book cover area is covered.

4. Turn the ½" border of the canvas under and stitch it down with heavy-duty thread.

5. Measure and cut the heavy interfacing to fit the back of the canvas.

6. Cut the fabric the size of the heavy interfacing plus 1" all around.

7. Fuse the fabric to one side of the interfacing; turn it over and iron the edges of the fabric to the back of the interfacing.

8. Cut nine 8 ½" x 6" pieces of interfacing to create three signatures for a total of thirty-six pages.

9. Tint the pages with fluid acrylics and let them dry.

10. Stack three pages together and create three signatures (see Sewn-Signature Books, page 81). Stitch each signature to the book lining at the fold.

11. Hand-stitch the book lining with the signatures to the hooked cover.

A chapbook is an informal book in which you write original poetry, favorite quotes, or special recipes. In the nineteenth century, chapbooks were often sent to friends and family instead of Christmas or other types of holiday cards. Whatever you write or record, a sewn-signature chapbook like this one is so easy to make it can be the perfect gift for any occasion.

To create the cover background for *Chapbook* I used photo-editing software to copy and repeat a small pattern from the cover photo. I enlarged, enhanced, and added the cover photo, then printed my custom design onto inkjet-ready fabric. After I laminated the fabric, it was ready to be wrapped around the pages to form the front and back covers.

When a thing has been said, and said well, have no scruple. Take it and copy it.

~ Anatole France

Materials
Clear iron-on vinyl • Computer, scanner, and inkjet printer • Fabric • Fluid acrylic paints • Inkjet-ready fabric • Iron and ironing board • Iron-on fusible • Large needle • Medium weight interfacing • Paintbrushes • Permanent pen • Photos • Ribbon • Scissors or rotary cutter

Method

1. Scan and alter the cover art photograph for printing. Print it onto inkjet-ready fabric.

2. Using iron-on fusible, fuse the inside of the cover fabric to the outer book cover.

3. To laminate the cover, cut two pieces of clear iron-on vinyl that are larger than the cover fabric. Follow the manufacturer's directions to iron into place. Trim the excess.

4. Cut three 10 $\frac{1}{2}$" x 8 $\frac{1}{2}$" pieces of medium-weight interfacing. Tint the interfacing with fluid acrylics. Let it dry.

5. Stack three sheets of interfacing together and fold them in half to create one signature (see Signature Construction, page 30.) *Note: The signature will have six pages that are 5 $\frac{1}{4}$" x 8 $\frac{1}{2}$" at finished size.*

6. Attach the signature to the cover with ribbon and a large needle. Knot and tie the ends in a bow.

7. Inscribe the pages with quotes, recipes, or poetry.

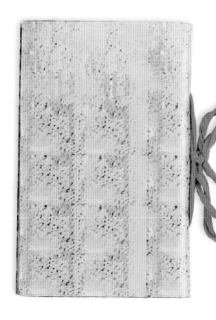

TEDDY BEAR

A book and a teddy bear—how often do you get to create two such wonderful things at one time? A simple nursery rhyme (teddy bear themed, of course!) becomes a deliciously tactile experience when you use faux fur, fleece, and interactive features bound with a sewn signature. Children of all ages love this book.

Imagine the delight your little one will have "reading" a teddy bear. Interactive features such as tiny bears that can be taken out and put back into a pocket will make cuddle time extra fun.

A bear teaches us that if the heart is true, it doesn't matter if an ear drops off.

~ Helen Exley

Materials

Acid-free mat board, 8" x 15" • Awl or large needle • Chalk • Copy of bear patterns (pages 98 & 101) • Curved needle • Ephemera • Fabric glue • Faux fur, ½ yard • Felt for pages, six pieces 7½" x 15" • Measuring tape or ruler • Pencil • Photos on fabric • Polyester stuffing • Scissors or rotary cutter • Sewing machine (optional) • Six-strand embroidery floss; black, neutral or brown • Stiff cardboard • Straight needle for embroidery floss • Strong thread • Two black shoe-button type eyes • Craft knife

Method

1. Determine the correct direction of the fur. Trace two bear heads from Pattern 1 (page 98) onto the back of the faux fur.

2. Cut out the patterns. Patterns include a seam allowance around all the pattern lines. Avoid cutting the strands of the faux fur.

3. With the front sides of the faux fur facing each other, sew the head pieces together, leaving bottom edge open. Turn them inside out.

4. Lightly stuff the ears and hand or machine stitch through both layers where the pattern lines indicate.

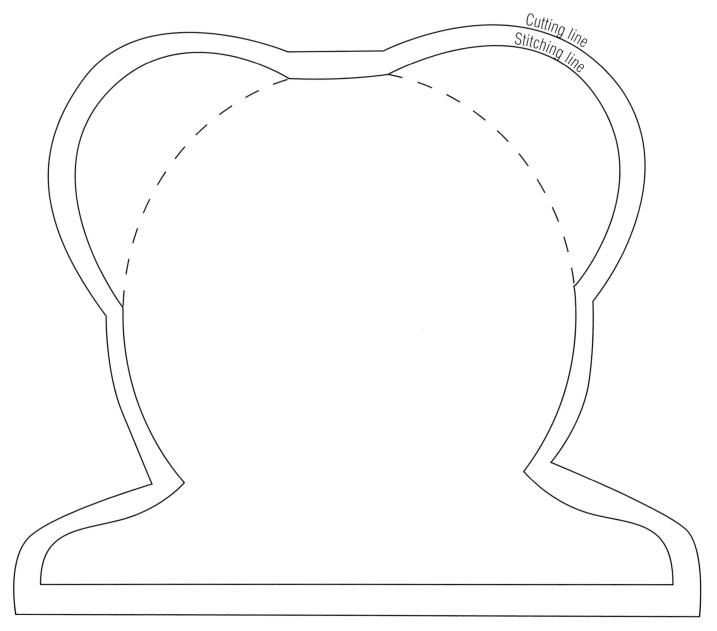

PATTERN 1.

5. Lay the head pattern at the top of the mat board and trace around it. Mark the dots from the pattern along the neck and add an additional 7" in length below the pattern's bottom edge for the book back and head reinforcement. Cut off the ears of the mat board head (see Diagram 2, page 100.)

6. Starting at the base of the shoulders, trim ½" from the mat board so that the head is ½" smaller all around to fit inside the stitched head.

7. On the back of the mat board, score a line ½" from each edge and bend both sides of the head board towards the center.

8. Insert the mat board into the head and flatten the edges. Continue to stuff and shape the head with polyester stuffing, giving some roundness to the front of the face.

9. Position the eyes and stitch them onto the face using a curved needle and heavy-duty thread or dental floss. Make the stitches deep into the stuffing and pull the eyes back into the head so they are slightly recessed and not sitting loosely on top. Knot and tie off the thread securely.

10. Lightly mark the nose area with chalk and stitch the nose using the curved needle, six-strand embroidery floss, and a satin stitch. (See Diagram 1.)

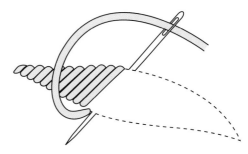

DIAGRAM 1. A satin stich is composed of parallel rows of straight stitches.

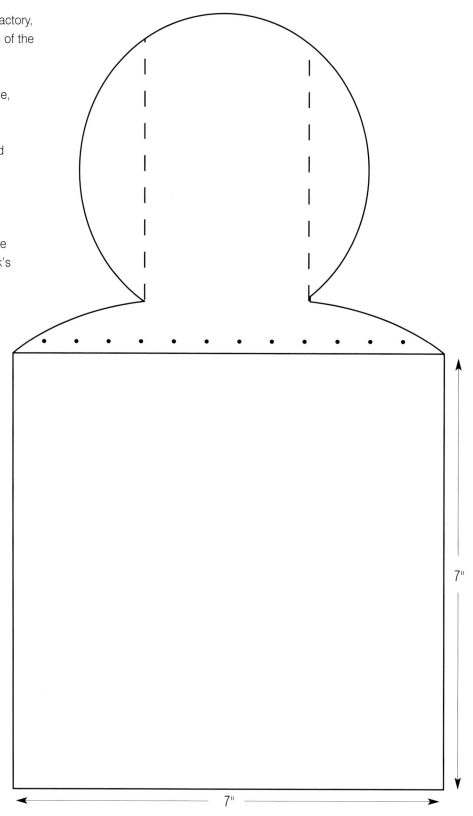

11. When the bear head is satisfactory, pull it securely toward the bottom of the mat board.

12. Using an awl or strong needle, punch holes into the mat board. (Refer to the dots on Diagram 2. Secure the head to the mat board by stitching through the holes using strong thread.

13. Make sure the fur direction matches the head and cut a piece of bear fur 7 3/4" x 15" for the book's back and cover.

14. Glue half of the cut piece of fur to the back of the mat board, overlapping the stitched neck area and leaving 1/2" to overlap the right edge of the mat board. *Note: Position the fur of the body so that the knap goes in the same direction as that of the fur on the head.*

DIAGRAM 2. Position Teddy Bear Pattern 1 over your mat board so that you can measure and cut a 7" square directly below the bear's head. Draw twelve evenly spaced dots between the bear's "shoulders" to indicate where you will punch holes as instructed in step 12.

7"

7"

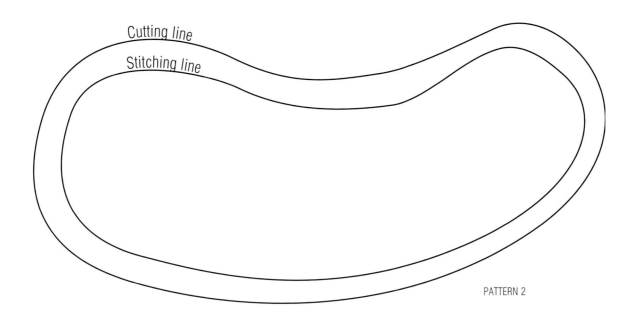

Cutting *line*

Stitching *line*

PATTERN 2

15. To create an arm, trace Teddy Bear Pattern 2 onto faux fur. Flip the pattern and trace again. Cut out the arm shapes and sew them together, fur side in, leaving an opening for turning and stuffing. Repeat to create the other arm. Turn the arms right-side-out, fill them with polyester stuffing, and hand stitch closed. Stitch the arms to the cover.

16. Open the cover. Cut a coordinating piece of felt 7 1/2" x 15" and glue it to the inside of the front cover and over the mat board, overlapping the stitched neck area and meeting the overlap on the right side, encasing the mat board.

17. Cut three pieces of felt (or similar weight fabric) 7" x 13 ½". Fold them over to create one signature totaling six pages.

18. Design the fabric collage layout for each page, keeping in mind the final layout. (See Signature Construction, page 30).

19. Stitch the collages onto each page. Because these are single layer pages, any stitching on one side of the page will show through to the other. As an option, glue or fuse the collage to the page.

20. Sew the signature into the bear book cover using embroidery floss.

A BEARY GOOD BOOK
by
LESLEY RILEY

Golden Classics

Alternative Books

So far we've talked about book construction techniques that require no binding and those that use accordion folds, buttons, and stitches. But of course there are many other ways to hold together the pages of your fabric memory books. This chapter covers a few more binding techniques with projects that use binder rings, tabs, sticks, and grommets.

Fan-Fold Books

A fan-fold book is made from several separate pages (single- or double-sided) that are joined together at one corner, allowing them to fan open. There are myriad ways to join the pages, including a post, ring, cord, or stitch. Choose one that fits the look and feel of the book and is strong enough to withstand the repeated opening and closing the book will endure when friends and family ooh and ahh over it. Just remember when you create the pages that you shouldn't put anything you want people to see in the corner where the pages will be bound.

The simplicity of a fan-fold binding doesn't mean it has to look simplistic. Bead-embellished ribbon makes this binding as decorative as it is functional.

Grommet or Eyelet Bindings

You can combine a grommet or eyelet binding with almost any book construction technique. In *Family* (page 110), I used them with binder rings in place of stitches after stacking pages the way I would to create a simple sewn binding. For *Bethany Beach* (page 112), I set the eyelets in the corners of separate pages and threaded cord through them to create an accordion-folded book.

Before you set grommets or eyelets, first make a hole in your material with a Japanese screw punch, an awl, sharp scissors, or a craft knife. Take care that the hole is not larger than the stem of your grommets or eyelets. To set, use a hand tool specially designed for grommets or eyelets, whichever you are working with, and be sure to work on a hard surface. Once all the grommets or eyelets are set, thread cord, ribbon, wire, or whatever suits your design through the reinforced holes and bind your book. If working with delicate fabric, consider reinforcing the fabric with interfacing or another layer of material and use eyelets, which are smaller and lighter than grommets.

Grommets and loose-leaf metal rings form a sturdy and attractive binding for a book you want many people to flip through and pass around.

A tab binding can be a dramatic design element that enables you to use the full space of your pages.

Tab Bindings

With most binding methods, a narrow margin of the page is hidden in the binding. Because a tab binding exposes every edge of the page, it's great when a traditional binding method won't work, when you want another design element, or when you don't want to lose any of the decorated page space. Tabs can be made from ribbon, tape, fabric or leather strips, or a fabric tube (a folded fabric strip sewn along one edge and turned inside-out). As you can see with the project *Follow* (page 118) creating a tab binding is simple: attach a set of tabs to each page, stack the pages, and attach the corresponding sets of tabs together. If you choose delicate materials for your tabs, I recommend a double layer.

Stick Bindings

Stick binding is a traditional bookbinding method in which the stitches that hold the pages go around a stick placed along the left edge of the front cover and the right edge of the back cover. As with the buttons in a button-binding, the sticks prevent the stitches from pulling through the fabric. They also lend some "spine" to a fabric memory book.

The paintbrushes used as the front and back sticks of *Young At Art* (page 115) prevent the stitches from pulling through the fabric, provide rigid support for the pages, and enhance the book's artistic theme.

To create a stick-bound book, line up your pages between the front and back covers. Lay one stick about ¼" from the left edge of the front cover and another stick about ¼" inch from the right edge of the back cover. If you wish, glue the sticks in place. Using a sturdy needle and a strong thread such as waxed linen, start at the center and stitch through the cover and all layers, around the stick on the back cover, and back up and over the stick on the front. If you have trouble pulling the needle through, use pliers to grasp and pull. Repeat the stitching in the same location to reinforce. Knot or tie off the tail of the thread. Repeat the process to bind the top and bottom of each stick about 1" from each end of the sticks.

MAMA

Some of my favorite images are those of my mama as a young girl. Because the originals are faded and yellow, I used photo-editing software to adjust the color and contrast and apply an edge-defining filter. The result is that the images have a more powerful presence against the brightly colored and patterned backgrounds in this fan-folded book than the original images would have.

For this project, I chose to collage on only one side of each page, allowing colorful fabrics to add interest to the other side. If you decide to collage on both sides, be sure to complete any collage sewing before joining the front and back layers to avoid stitching into the collage on the opposite side.

When I stopped seeing my mother with the eyes of a child, I saw the woman who helped me give birth to myself.

~ Nancy Friday

Materials

A selection of fabrics • Batting • Buttons and other embellishments • Fabric strips, ribbon, or seam binding • Inkjet-ready fabric • Needle nose pliers • Needle with large eye • Photos • Pliers (optional) • Ribbon • Scissors or rotary cutter • Sewing machine (optional)

Method

1. For each page, cut two pieces of fabric the desired page size.

2. Cut a piece of batting for each page slightly smaller than the page size so that it is hidden between the fabric layers.

3. Print photos onto inkjet-ready fabric (see page 20). Create a photo and fabric collage on each page. Hand or machine stitch through all the layers to create a quilted page.

4. If creating a collage on the page front and back, stitch or fuse each one separately before adding batting and joining all the layers.

5. Choose a method for finishing the edges:
Option 1: Machine zigzag around all four edges of the page. Trim the outer edges to the stitching.
Option 2: Turn under the edges of the fabric and hand or machine stitch them closed.
Option 3: Bind the edges with single-fold seam binding, ribbon, or fabric strips and sew or fuse them in place.

6. Join pages together at one corner using a needle and ribbon. *Note: Use pliers to grasp and pull the needle through each page if necessary.*

7. Tie a knot around beads, balls, or buttons as a stop to hold the ribbon in place on the front and back.

BOOK smarts

If joining pages with a post, ring, or cord, reinforce the holes with grommets or eyelets for added durability.

FAMILY

During a family vacation, I threw a huge pile of fabric onto the table and invited my family to dive in and create personal pages. Everyone got into it, from my 85-year-old father, Jack, to my three-year-old grandson, Jack. Each person chose three to five fabrics to create a fabric collage page that I later assembled into the grommet-bound book you see here.

Collaborative memory books are a great way to involve people near and dear to you. To make sure it really happens, be prepared for on-the-spot creativity at the next gathering. While my family was playing with fabric, I took each person aside to snap a digital photo that I printed then and there using a portable photo printer and inkjet-ready fabric cut to size.

Do not the most moving moments of our lives find us all without words?

~ Marcel Marceau

Materials
Digital camera and photo printer • Fabric for page backgrounds • Fabric scraps for collage • Grommets and grommet setting tool • Inkjet-ready fabric • Iron and ironing board • Iron-on fusible • Loose-leaf rings • Permanent pen for people to sign pages (optional) • Sewing needle • Straight pins • Thread

Method

1. Take a portrait photo of each person participating in the book project. Print the photos on inkjet-ready fabric (see page 20). Back the fabric with iron-on fusible before cutting out the photos.

2. Provide a generous amount of fabric for the group to choose from. Instruct them to pick three to five fabrics each, with one large enough for a background of approximately 8" x 10".

3. Let each person lay out his or her collage and pin it in place. Remind everyone to leave a 1" border around the collages to accommodate the binding.

4. Stitch or fuse each collage into place.

5. Place two pages back-to-back and fuse or stitch them together around all four edges.

6. Create the front and back covers. Decorate the front cover, then fuse or stitch another piece of fabric to it to create the inside cover.

7. Set grommets in the cover and in each page. Start 1" from the top and bottom, and center one or two more in between, depending on the page size.

8. Join the pages with loose-leaf rings.

BETHANY BEACH 2005

To get pictures perfect for a beach-themed fabric memory book, I asked my family to dress in white and neutral colors. The limited palette created unity between the photos and worked well with the overall design of the book, which encases collages between softly luminous sheets of mica.

To better align the photos from page to page, I cropped them to the same size. This enabled me to stitch around the edges of the mica without going through any of the photos.

You create the opportunity for magic only by giving up your preconceptions.

~ Toinette Lippe

Materials
Assorted fabric scraps • Craft or silicone glue • Embellishments • Eyelets, ⅛" • Eyelet setting tool • Hole punch, ⅛", and an awl, or Japanese screw punch, 3.5 mm • Paperclips • Pencil • Photos printed on fabric • Polyester thread • Sewing machine with small needle • Six to ten large sheets of mica • Twine, yarn, or ribbon

Method

1. Prepare two sheets of mica for every book panel.

2. Create small fabric and photo collages and sandwich them between mica sheets.

3. Place paperclips on each side to hold the mica sandwiches in place.

4. Machine stitch the sandwiches together using a small needle and polyester thread, removing the paperclips one at a time. *Note: Mica shreds rayon and metallic thread.*

BOOK smarts

To prepare mica for machine sewing, split a sheet into layers that are about the depth of an index card—any thinner and the mica is prone to breakage. Start at one edge and slide your fingernail or a craft knife between the layers. Gently move around the perimeter of the mica sheet and, as the edges separate, carefully pull the layers apart. Trim the thinner sheets to size using a straight edge and a craft knife. Save the scraps for other projects. If you find separating mica sheets to be challenging, keep trying. With practice, you'll gain skill and a wonderful element to add to your fabric books.

5. Mark a corner for each eyelet without getting too close to the edge. Punch a hole the same size as each eyelet. If the fabric extends to the corner of the sandwich, punch the hole through it using a Japanese screw punch or an awl.

6. Using an eyelet setting tool, set the eyelets. Work on a very hard surface for greater ease.

7. Thread twine, ribbon, or yarn through the eyelets and tie it together.

8. Glue embellishments to the cover.

YOUNG AT ART

It was Arts Night at Bethesda Elementary. The school was a gallery with all the walls covered by art. When I came across the second grade's work, I envisioned a wall in my house covered with these colorful self-portraits. Because I couldn't buy each and every one of them, I did the next best thing—I asked permission to scan them and create a book to share with you. And here it is!

Perhaps you have a little someone in your life who makes wonderful art. Collect those masterpieces in a fabric memory book you can thumb through for years to come.

Henry Doran

Arielle Bleeker

Every child is an artist. The problem is how to remain an artist once he grows up.

~ Pablo Picasso

Materials Acrylic gesso • Acrylic paints • Clamps • Colorful cotton thread, #3 • Crewel needle • Inkjet-ready fabric • Measuring tape or ruler • Paintbrushes • Scanned artwork • Scissors or rotary cutter • Sewing needle • Straight pins • Thread • Two paintbrushes, pencils, or sticks • Unstretched painters canvas or cotton duck

Method

1. Print the artwork onto inkjet-ready fabric at the full size of the fabric sheet (see page 20). Trim off the white margin, if there is one.

2. Cut as many pages as desired from the unstretched canvas or duck. Paint both sides of each page with gesso. Let the pages dry.

3. Stack the pages and measure them for the cover size. Cut a piece of unstretched canvas or duck for the cover. Paint only the exterior of the cover with gesso.

4. Using colors that complement the artwork, paint splotches of acrylic paint on the outside edges of each page. Let the pages dry.

5. Place the artwork printed on fabric on both sides of each page. Use a straight pin to align the corners of the fabric on the front and back of each page. Pin the fabric in place.

6. Stitch around the artwork on one side of a page, catching the edges of the artwork on the back. Flip the page over and stitch it down from the opposite side if a section is missed. Repeat until all pages are completed.

7. Decorate the cover.

Semir Michael   **Katherine Garcia**

Katie Kleinknecht

Madeline Martinez

8. Stack the pages and place the cover over the stack. Make the pages snug against the inside cover. Clamp the pages and the cover together to hold them in place.

9. Glue a paintbrush or similar item about ¹/₂" from the left edge of the front cover. Clamp it in place until the glue dries. Repeat to attach the second brush ¹/₂" from the right edge of the back cover.

10. Once the brushes are glued in place, stitch over them through all the layers using cotton thread and a crewel needle to bind the book (see Stick Bindings, page 105.)

FOLLOW

To make the pages of this tab-bound book more than a backdrop for the art, I kept the collage to a minimum and added plenty of color and texture to the spun-bonded polyester medium. Because I didn't want a binding that would infringe on the pages, I stitched a tab to each page and bound the tabs to each other.

When artist Virginia Spiegel shared her method of working with spun-bonded polyester—a type of industrial interfacing—in the premiere issue of *Cloth Paper Scissors*, I was smitten. I'm always looking for fabric that acts like paper and then some, and this one can be painted, burned, written on, and sewn. What more could a fabric-bookmaking girl want?

Follow your bliss and the universe will open doors for you where there were only walls.

~Joseph Campbell

Materials
Assorted trims and embellishments • Buttons or beads for binding • Craft soldering iron with pencil tip • Fabric assortment • Fabric glue • Fluid acrylic paints • Heavy-duty thread • Inkjet-ready fabric • Iron and ironing board • Iron-on fusible • Spun-bonded polyester • Paintbrushes • Photos • Quotes • Scissors or rotary cutter • Sewing needle • Straight pins • Wood block

Method

1. Cut spun-bonded polyester to the approximate page size. Don't try for uniformity in size—keep it random.

2. Paint spun-bonded polyester with fluid acrylics and let it dry. Iron the fabric to heat-set the paint.

3. Working in a well-ventilated area, burn holes and create interesting edges in the spun-bonded polyester using a craft soldering iron with a pencil tip. Clean the tip often by rubbing it on a wood block.

4. Print the photos and quotes onto inkjet-ready fabric (see page 20). Apply iron-on fusible to the back of the fabric. Cut out the images and quotes.

5. Create fabric and photo collages on the cover and on each page. Fuse them in place.

6. To create tabs for the binding, cut a 2 ¼" wide length of fabric the desired length. Fold the fabric lengthwise and stitch a tube with a ¼" seam. Turn the tube inside out and cut 3" lengths for tabs.

7. Fold each tab over the edge of a page and pin it in place, making sure to keep the pages aligned as you work on them. Stitch each tab down about ½" from the page edge.

8. Stack the pages together and, with heavy-duty thread, stitch through each tab using a button or bead on the front and back of each tab stack as decorative elements.

Metric Conversion Chart

INCHES	METRIC (MM/CM)	INCHES	METRIC (MM/CM)	INCHES	METRIC (MM/CM)	INCHES	METRIC (MM/CM)	INCHES	METRIC (MM/CM)
$1/16$	1.6 mm	$2^1/_2$	6.4 cm	$11^1/_2$	29.2 cm	$20^1/_2$	52 cm	$29^1/_2$	74.9 cm
$1/8$	3 mm	3	7.6 cm	12	30.5 cm	21	53.3	30	76.2 cm
$3/16$	5 mm	$3^1/_2$	8.9 cm	$12^1/_2$	31.8 cm	$21^1/_2$	54.6	$30^1/_2$	77.5 cm
$1/4$	6 mm	4	10.2 cm	13	33 cm	22	55 cm	31	78.7 cm
$5/16$	8 mm	$4^1/_2$	11.4 cm	$13^1/_2$	34.3 cm	$22^1/_2$	57.2 cm	$31^1/_2$	80 cm
$3/8$	9.5 mm	5	12.7 cm	14	35.6 cm	23	58.4 cm	32	81.3 cm
$7/16$	1.1 cm	$5^1/_2$	14 cm	$14^1/_2$	36.8 cm	$23^1/_2$	59.7 cm	$32^1/_2$	82.6 cm
$1/2$	1.3 cm	6	15.2 cm	15	38.1 cm	24	61 cm	33	83.8 cm
$9/16$	1.4 cm	$6^1/_2$	16.5 cm	$15^1/_2$	39.4 cm	$24^1/_2$	62.2 cm	$33^1/_2$	85 cm
$5/8$	1.6 cm	7	17.8 cm	16	40.6 cm	25	63.5 cm	34	86.4 cm
$11/16$	1.7 cm	$7^1/_2$	19 cm	$16^1/_2$	41.9 cm	$25^1/_2$	64.8 cm	$34^1/_2$	87.6 cm
$3/4$	1.9 cm	8	20.3 cm	17	43.2 cm	26	66 cm	35	88.9 cm
$13/16$	2.1 cm	$8^1/_2$	21.6 cm	$17^1/_2$	44.5 cm	$26^1/_2$	67.3 cm	$35^1/_2$	90.2 cm
$7/8$	2.2 cm	9	22.9 cm	18	45.7 cm	27	68.6 cm	36	91.4 cm
$15/16$	2.4 cm	$9^1/_2$	24.1 cm	$18^1/_2$	47 cm	$27^1/_2$	69.9 cm	$36^1/_2$	92.7 cm
1	2.5 cm	10	25.4 cm	19	48.3 cm	28	71.1 cm	37	94.0 cm
$1^1/_2$	3.8 cm	$10^1/_2$	26.7 cm	$19^1/_2$	49.5 cm	$28^1/_2$	72.4 cm	$37^1/_2$	95.3 cm
2	5 cm	11	27.9 cm	20	50.8 cm	29	73.7 cm	38	96.5 cm

Notes on Suppliers

Usually, the supplies you need for making the projects in Lark books can be found at your local craft supply store, discount mart, home improvement center, or retail shop relevant to the topic of the book. Occasionally, however, you may need to buy materials or tools from specialty suppliers. In order to provide you with the most up-to-date information, we have created a list of suppliers on our website, which we update on a regular basis. Visit us at www.larkbooks.com, click on "Craft Supply Sources," and then click on the relevant topic. You will find numerous companies listed with their web address and/or mailing address and phone number.

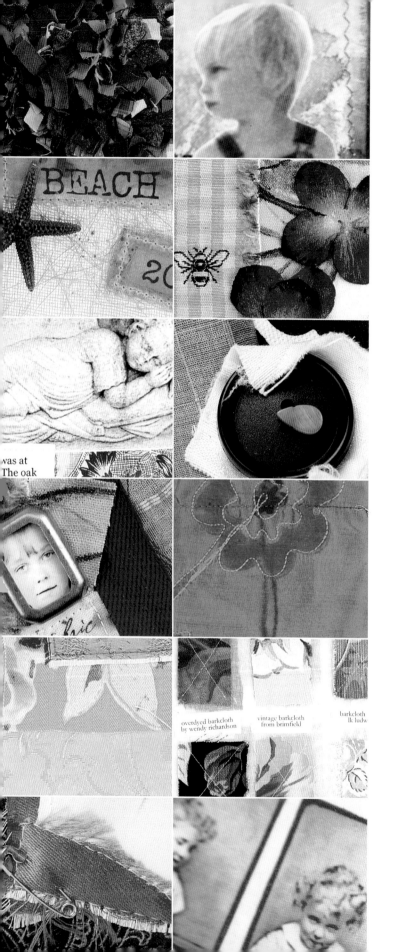

overdyed barkcloth
by wendy richardson

vintage barkcloth
from brimfield

barkcloth
lk ludw

Acknowledgments

This book, like any other, is a group effort. Many people behind the scenes whose names I will never know were instrumental in placing this book in readers' hands. Though you are not named here, please know that I appreciate the part you played in making this book a reality.

I would like to thank Jo Packham of Chapelle, Ltd. for the opportunity to write another book before the first one was even printed. Her confidence in me as an artist and author was a guiding light in working on this book. Paige Gilchrist, Senior Editor at Lark Books, took this project under her wing and flew it safely to its completion. I am thankful for the care and attention she gave to get this book to your hands.

My editors, Jennifer Gibbs and David Macfarlane, have disproved the saying that too many cooks spoil the broth. Working together, we have refined my words to make this book easier for you to read and understand. The work and vision of 828, Inc. and Zac Williams have made the book a visual delight as well.

My friends and fellow artists responded enthusiastically to a call for contributions for the boxed portfolio book *Home*. Their participation made this book richer in both art and spirit, and I'm sure this donation will help the organization First Book raise funds for providing children with much-needed books of their own. Thank you!

My students also deserve thanks and recognition here. Sometimes I wonder who is teaching whom. Their unending enthusiasm and fresh eyes inspire me and keep my own work alive and new. Special thanks go to Darlene Troyer for sharing her photographs and talent with me, and for making the *Stone Angels* fabric book possible.

Writing a book is a labor of love, but it also takes time away from those you love. At times my family, Kelly in particular, had to take a backseat to timelines and deadlines. My deepest thanks go to my mother and father, Jack and June; my husband, Buddy; and my most outstanding creations—my children: Kelly, Kerry, Samantha, Chris, Sara, and Brian (Amy, Emma, Annie, Jack, and Kathryn too). I stole time from you in order to write this book. I can think of nothing better than making up for lost time.

About the Author

Lesley Riley is a mixed-media artist who has worked with fabric for over thirty years and is the author of *Quilted Memories* (Sterling/Chapelle, 2005). She teaches quilting, bookmaking, and mixed-media workshops internationally and is the Arts Editor for *Cloth Paper Scissors*. Lesley is a sixth generation Washingtonian (DC) and a mother of six. She welcomes questions and comments from readers and can be reached via her website at www.lalasland.com.

Contributors

The following artists generously created pages for the project *Home* (page 42) as part of a donation to First Book, a non-profit organization dedicated to promoting literacy.

Nina Bagley

With such designs as "booklaces"–miniature books that double as wearable art-teacher, professional jewelry designer, and mixed media artist Nina Bagley inspires artists to seek innovative ways to use materials and bend genres. Her art has appeared in several publications, including *Cloth, Paper, Scissors; Somerset Studio;* and *Mary Englebreit's Home Companion*; yet her two sons and her home in the Smoky Mountain foothills are her greatest source of pride. www.ninabagley.com

Sas Colby

For more than thirty years, Sas Colby has been making art and traveling to share her expertise with students at such locales as the Anderson Ranch Arts Center in Colorado, the Haystack Mountain School in Maine, the Penland School in North Carolina, and universities in the US and Australia. Each summer she leads an art retreat in Taos, New Mexico. Her work is in international collections including France's Bibliotheque Nationale, the National Gallery of Australia, and the Women's Museum in Washington, DC. www.sascolby.com

Patti Culea

Patti Culea's work has been featured in several books and magazines in the US and the UK, including *Soft Dolls & Animals, Art Doll Quarterly, Cloth Paper Scissors*, and *Quilting Arts*. Best known for her unique style of doll making, Patti also designs journal patterns, has developed her own approach to beadwork, and teaches classes internationally. www.PMCDesigns.com

Claire Waguespack Fenton

As a lifelong resident of southern Louisiana, Claire's work has been influenced by the region's lush semi-tropical landscape, the rich cultural heritage of the area, and, more recently, the reality of the natural and manmade events that threaten its survival. Her deeply expressive work is created from fabrics that have been hand painted and dyed (frequently with rust) and is typically heavily stitched. She has won numerous regional and national awards in both art and quilting venues. www.clairefenton.com

Mary Fisher

Mary Fisher's artwork includes quilts, sculptures, photography, paintings, and more. The former television producer and advisor to President Gerald Ford is a passionate advocate and well-known speaker on the global AIDS epidemic. Her quilt exhibit *Abataka* combines fabric art with photography and excerpts from interviews with AIDS patients and their caregivers, and has been called "powerful and compassionate" by critics. The artist has also authored several books, including *Angels in Our Midst, My Name is Mary: A Memoir*, and *I'll Not Go Quietly*. www.maryfisher.com.

Claudine Hellmuth

Nationally known collage artist Claudine Hellmuth approaches collage the old-fashioned way, cutting, pasting, and painting by hand. In addition to creating art full time, the Florida-based artist teaches mixed media collage workshops in the US and Canada, has authored the books *Collage Discovery Workshop* and *Collage Discovery Workshop: Beyond the Unexpected*, and has produced two instructional DVD workshops. In 2004, she was a guest on the Carol Duvall show on HGTV demonstrating techniques from her book. www.collageartist.com

Karen Michel

Mixed media artist Karen Michel lives in New York where she and her husband run the Creative Art Space for Kids Foundation, a non-profit art center for children. Her books, paintings, and collages have been exhibited internationally and have appeared in various publications, including her book *The Complete Guide to Altered Imagery*. www.karenmichel.com

Lynne Perrella

As an artist, Lynne is drawn to collage, assemblage, art journals, and one-of-a-kind books. Her art and articles have appeared in various publications on mixed media, including her books *Artists' Journals & Sketchbooks, Alphabetica*, and *Beyond Paper Dolls*. She is on the editorial advisory boards of *Somerset Studio* and *Legacy*, conducts creativity workshops internationally, and exhibits her work at galleries throughout the Berkshires. www.LKPerrella.com

Susan Shie

Susan Shie has been an artist all her life, telling stories through drawing, painting, writing, and sewing. Her Outsider Art Quilts are a mixture of personal diary and her reflections on the world. Themes in her work include the relationship between the personal and political (and vice versa). "I now consider America to be our Garden of Freedoms," says Shie, "and we must love it or weed it. Family is all-important, and the whole world is our Family to love and care for." www.turtlemoon.com

Laura Wasilowski

Laura's contemporary art quilts, made from fused fabrics and machine stitching, combine stories of family, friends, and home with the inspiration of unique fabrics, many of which Laura stamps, paints, or dyes herself. The combination of fabric and story results in pictorial quilts that chronicle her life. In addition to exhibiting her work internationally, Laura owns the dye shop, Artfabrik, and is a lecturer, surface designer, quilt instructor, and author of *Fusing Fun: Fast, Fearless Art Quilts*. www.artfabrik.com

Lynne Whipple

Multi media artist Lynne Whipple approaches her work in a spirit of play. As she combines such items as found objects, old books, and memorabilia, she gravitates toward images that strike her as "slightly absurd." The Florida resident's art has appeared in numerous publications and can be found in galleries and collections worldwide. www.WhippleArt.com

Index